ODI Development Policy Studies

A Reaction Too Far

Economic theory and the role of the state in developing countries

Tony K

GW01066373

Overseas Development Institute

Acknowledgements

Preparation of this monograph was undertaken while I was on sabbatical leave. I would like to thank the Council of ODI for giving me this opportunity, and Wolfson College and the Department of Applied Economics, University of Cambridge, for making their facilities open to me. I must also thank John Cathie, Sidney Dell, Gerald Helleiner, Sheila Page, Roger Riddell, Michael Roemer, Frances Stewart, Mary Tiffen and John Toye for valuable comments on earlier drafts. An earlier version of this paper was commissioned by the Overseas Development Administration and I am grateful for their support of this project. Responsibility for the views expressed here is, of course, mine alone.

TK.

British Library Cataloguing in Publication Data:

Killick, Tony
    A reaction too far: economic theory and the role of the state in developing countries
    1. Developing countries. Economic policies
    I. Title
    330.9172′4

    ISBN 0-85003-147-8

© Overseas Development Institute 1989, 1990
Reprinted October 1990 with revised preface

Published by the Overseas Development Institute,
Regent's College, Inner Circle, Regent's Park, London NW1 4NS

Printed and typeset by the Russell Press Ltd, Nottingham

Contents

Preface

Implications of the Collapse of Communism

The essay that follows was written during the first half of 1988. Since then the world has witnessed the dramatic collapse of communism in much of Eastern Europe and its replacement, where multi-party elections have been held, by more or less conservative governments pledged to the establishment of market economies. Thus, at an April 1990 meeting of the Conference on Security and Co-operation in Europe all the East European governments, *including that of the Soviet Union*, pledged themselves to endeavour to achieve competitive market economies where prices are based on supply and demand and to recognise the right to own private property. At the very least, such events make up a remarkable change in attitudes towards the state as an economic agent and in the environment within which its economic role should be considered. It may, therefore, be of interest to speculate on what further implications these changes may have for the subject matter of this essay.

First, it seems inevitable that there will be major after-the-event revisions of Marxist and neo-Marxist theories of economic organisation and policy. An aspect of events in Eastern Europe that has tended to be overshadowed by the displays of people power is that much of the momentum for change there came from reformers *within* the ruling communist parties. It appears there was a cumulative realisation both of the increasing gravity of the economic problems confronted and of the inability of existing systems of central planning and control to solve them. It is this decline in the intellectual self-confidence of Marxist economists — which can be linked to the revision of orthodoxy in favour of market solutions that has been under way for some time (noted on p.17 below) — which seems to guarantee sweeping further revisions, as well as defections from Marxian orthodoxy as it has been practised in the past.

Even now there no longer exists any working model of a systematic, intellectually plausible alternative to capitalism as the dominant mode of production. The movement in favour of reducing the role of the state and of entrusting more economic decisions to the marketplace has received a powerful boost. Developing country governments still espousing hard- or soft-line command economy approaches look stranded, not only geo-politically but also intellectually. Some of them are already engaged in re-thinking and are moving towards democratisation.

With many Second and Third World governments looking afresh at the design of economic policy, the collapse of communism increases the danger of the 'reaction too far' with which this essay is concerned. Such a change in the environment appears unfavourable to the pragmatic approach to the roles of the state and of markets advocated on the following pages. At the same time, the virtual disappearance of capitalism's competing ideology — what has rather fancifully been called 'the end of history' — may take some of the passion out of the subject, leaving ideologues *of both persuasions* with less wind in their sails. It may become actually easier to be guided by careful judgements about costs and benefits.

This may be reinforced by the nature of the transitional problems which erstwhile socialist economies, Second and Third World, will encounter in their conversion to market-based economies. It seems from the results of most multi-party elections held so far that the electorates of Eastern Europe have rejected a compromise strategy of creating some kind of hybrid 'social market', opting instead for going all the way to a market economy. The problem with this is that economics has little advice to offer on how to effect the transition from a command to a market economy. One reason for this is provided by the theory of the second-best. This is discussed briefly on p.29 below where it is suggested that a pragmatic, case-by-case strategy is the best approach to policy when seeking to improve upon situations of many large distortions in the economy.

It may well also be that governments seeking to make this transition should particularly bear in mind the distinction made below between decisions about the desirable *size* of the state in economic life and the *forms of its interventions* in the economy. There is clearly going to be a change in both, in favour of interventions that operate through market forces and in favour of a smaller state sector, e.g. through privatisations. But decisions about size and about forms are not synonymous and there may be a danger of attributing to size ill-effects which are, in fact, the result of inappropriate types of intervention.

Finally, there may be some mutual learning to be done about policy design between the 'structural adjustment' programmes currently under way in many developing countries and the programmes of economic reform being embarked upon in Eastern Europe. One strategic question which has long troubled the former group is now one of the key issues confronting the latter: whether to approach policy reform by a 'short sharp shock' approach or in a more gradual way.[1] More generally, the economics of transition from heavily distorted to market economies has emerged as a subject area urgently in need of more research, from which both groups of countries stand to benefit.

April 1990   **T.K.**

---

1. For an advocacy of the radical option for Eastern Europe see the article by Jeffrey Sachs in *The Economist*, 13 January 1990, pp.23-28.

"The lesson, it seems to me, that we should draw from the history of economic thought is that economists should resist the pressure to embrace a one-sided or restrictive consensus. There is no one kind of economic truth which holds the key to fruitful analysis of all economic problems, no pure economic theory that is immune to changes in social values or current policy problems."
Phyllis Deane

1
Introduction

Important changes have been occurring in economic theory. These have been accompanied — at both theoretical and political levels — by a sharply reduced faith in the efficacy of policy interventions and an assertion of the superiority of market solutions. The Keynesian consensus in macroeconomics has broken down and the macro-micro distinction has become increasingly blurred. There has been much work to bring trade theory more in line with modern developments in international commerce; there have been important theoretical developments in the analysis of market efficiency and in welfare economics, as also in the theory of economic policy.

These changes in the theoretical core of the discipline have, of course, also influenced development economics. This now displays scepticism about the effects of planning and controls, and increasingly asserts the efficacy of market-oriented policies. At the same time, there is greater uncertainty about the rationale for, and future of, development economics itself, as the influence upon it of mainstream theory increases.[1]

The purposes of this monograph are to provide a guided tour of some relatively recent developments in economic theory, to examine the implications of these for the economic role of the state in developing countries [ldcs] and to briefly consider what inferences might be drawn for the policies of aid donors. 'Recent' is used loosely here, referring mainly to the 1970s and 1980s but

---

1. Thus, Albert Hirschman, 1982, has written of the 'rise and decline of development economics' and others see it as in crisis. This topic is the subject of Killick, 1988.

going further back in time where that seems helpful and I have been frequently reminded that many 'new' insights have antecedents going far back in the history of our discipline. Since there is a large literature to be surveyed in what is intended to be a succinct treatment, the discussion is conducted both in the main text and in extensive use of footnotes. The reader may wish to confine him/herself to the main text, at least for a first reading, referring only to the notes where elaboration or citations are desired. There is also an extensive bibliography, intended as an aid for readers who wish to follow up particular topics.

The argument that follows can be summarised in four propositions, which also broadly define the structure of the monograph:

(1) The major swing that has occurred in thinking about the nature and role of the state, although well founded in many respects, has gone too far and a correction is now under way.

(2) The most important questions about the role of the state are not How Big? or How Much? but What Kind? What Comparative Advantage? How Can State Performance Be Improved?

(3) In considering its policy recommendations we should be sensitive to the shaky or narrow theoretical foundations of much contemporary normative economics, especially when applied to ldcs.

(4) Contemporary thinking does offer valuable insights into aspects of policy in ldcs but there are no panaceas, no grounds for dogmatism. Aid donors should encourage experimental, tailor-made approaches to the design of policies in recipient countries.

2
The Reaction: Changing Views on the Role of the State

Theoretical shifts

That the 1980s have witnessed a major disillusionment with the state as an economic agent — by economists scarcely less than politicians — is an assertion that scarcely needs elaboration. Fiscal policies have come to be seen as creating major disincentives; attempts at macroeconomic management as destabilising or doomed to impotence; state attempts to plan, regulate and control as distorting the economy and spawning parallel markets; publicly-owned enterprises as inefficient and incapable of adequate self-improvement. However, it is important for present purposes to trace the developments within economic theory which led to this turning-away of the discipline from the *dirigisme* of earlier decades.

A very important contributor to this shift, of course, was the breakdown of the Keynesian consensus and the associated rise of the monetarist and rational expectations schools. With its commitment to full employment, orthodox Keynesianism proved unable to cope with the inflation that became increasingly rapid during the 1970s. The postulated Phillips curve[2] relationship between unemployment and inflation seemed increasingly to break down, with accelerating inflation becoming associated with a slow-down in economic growth and actual increases in the trend rate of unemployment — a situation of 'stagflation' with which most incomes policies could not deal and to which received macro

---

2. On this see Phillips, 1958, and Lipsey, 1960.

theory seemed to have little response.[3] It became increasingly apparent that wage negotiators were beginning to anticipate both future inflation and government policies, destroying the stability [and thus the usefulness] of the Phillips curve relationship and introducing the distinction between anticipated and unanticipated policy actions which became one of the pillars of rational expectations theory. While it may be justified to ignore the influence of expectations in the short run, it is not so over the longer term, as people have time to adjust to — and begin to anticipate — government actions, so part of the criticism of Keynesianism was, in effect, that its orientation was too short-term.

Keynesian treatment of time came to be further criticised on the additional ground that it tended to overlook the complications for policy of introducing time lags, as well as the complex interactions between policy instruments and the economic variables they are seeking to influence. Introducing these interactions and lead times (a) between the occurrence of a change in economic conditions and information about it, (b) between receipt of that information and the introduction of policy actions to correct for that change, and (c) between the introduction of a policy and its effect on the economy, can easily mean that measures intended to be stabilising turn out to have the opposite result. An assertion of this was a main part of Milton Friedman's onslaught on Keynesianism (1970 p.24).

Its emphasis on demand management and relative neglect of supply-side conditions provided a further stick with which the Keynesian consensus could be beaten, not the least because of the large supply shocks that were experienced in the 1970s, particularly via petroleum prices. There is today wide agreement on the importance of the supply side for the macroeconomic performance of an economy and much contemporary policy is intended to influence supply variables through the manipulation of pecuniary incentives.[4]

First monetarism, then rational expectations (RE), then the 'new classical' macroeconomics (NCM) came forward to fill the vacuum

---

3. See Vines 1986 and 1987 for useful discussions of these developments and their implications for macroeconomic analysis.

4. Fischer, 1988 p.330, has gone further to suggest that the greater microeconomic content of modern macroeconomics has undermined the notion that any standard macro model can have general applicability.

left by the attack on Keynesianism. The monetarist position is summarised by Friedman's famous dictum that "Inflation is always and everywhere a monetary phenomenon... and can be produced only by a more rapid increase in the quantity of money than in output", and by his associated denial that monetary expansion can result in any sustained increase in real output.[5] It sees fiscal expansion as merely 'crowding out' private sector expenditures, with reduction in the latter tending to negate the intended effects of a fiscal stimulus. It does not, however, completely deny the possibility of deflationary unemployment, and in advocating a policy of expanding money supply at a steady rate it envisages a benign influence of government policies on economic stability.

The RE school takes the analysis further and one of its attractions is that it applies to macroeconomic issues the same assumptions of rational maximising behaviour which underlie standard micro theory.[6] In particular, it applies them to the acquisition and processing of information and to the formation of expectations. It argues, for example in its critique of Phillips curve analysis, that economic agents will learn from past mistakes and come to anticipate systematic government policies, thus rendering them impotent. Only unexpected policies are able to influence real variables.

The NCM school take the analysis a step further, combining rational expectations with 'natural rate' theories of unemployment. In fact, disagreements about the nature of unemployment and the extent, or possibility, of deflationary unemployment have been a sub-plot in the macroeconomic controversies described here. The disagreement is largely about whether the labour market clears or not and, if so, how quickly. Natural-rate unemployment is essentially voluntary, although it also includes unemployment arising from frictional and structural causes. The NCM school sees the labour market as clearing almost instantly through the movement of wages and prices. Since, therefore, it is in equilibrium, any remaining unemployment must be voluntary, at least for the labour force considered collectively. A policy implication of this view is that, contrary to the Keynesian position,

---

5. Friedman, 1970, p.24.
6. For key expositions of the RE model see Lucas and Prescott, 1971, and Lucas, 1976. Shaw, 1984, provides a clear non-technical introduction and Maddock and Carter, 1982, offer a lively "child's guide".

unemployment cannot be reduced by demand expansion.[7] This conclusion is in line with a general denial by the NCM school of any possible influence on the economy of demand management policies, emphasising instead the importance of tax incentives and other measures to improve the efficiency of the labour market.[8]

These more recent contributions to macro theory are nevertheless deeply pessimistic about the feasibility of effective macroeconomic management and in this way have contributed importantly to a generally more jaundiced view of the effects of government policy interventions. By analogy with the concept of 'market failure' (discussed shortly) there is now far greater emphasis on the extent of 'government failure,' and the existence of a market failure is no longer accepted as constituting a case for intervention. The reasons can be summarised as follows:[9]

(a) The government is not necessarily well informed about the nature of a given problem, nor about the complex consequences of its own policy actions, which may produce perverse or unwanted effects. National planning has the effect of magnifying any mistakes or unwanted effects, as compared with the more limited effects of mistakes by individual economic agents in the marketplace.[10]

(b) Governments, in any case, have only partial control over the consequences of their actions.

(c) There are often large differences between policy measures on the drawing board and the way they are implemented. There are large intrinsic difficulties in improving the accountability and control of bureaucracies, and the problem is worsened both by the existence of corruption, nepotism and other malpractices and by the tendency for state agencies to be "captured" by special interest groups.

(d) Since lump-sum taxes, which do not affect incentives at the

---

7. See Friedman, 1968, and Phelps, 1967, 1970, for expositions.

8. For statements of this theory see Lucas and Sargent, 1981; Lucas, 1977; and Sargent, 1982. McCallum, 1980, offers a 'proof' of the impossibility of policies affecting real variables.

9. See Stiglitz, 1986 for a non-technical discussion of modern theories of public economics.

10. On this see Lal, 1983 p.74 and passim. This book provides an example of an anti-interventionist polemic, applied specifically to ldcs, which reflects aspects of present-day conservative economic thinking.

margin, are invariably not available to governments, any increase in taxation necessitated as a result of a policy intervention will itself introduce new 'distortions' by affecting relative prices and incentives.

Theories of rent-seeking and directly unproductive profit-seeking activities (DUPs) have added further strings to this bow.[11] Common examples include efforts by businessmen to secure allocations of import licenses, and the scarcity premia they will earn, and to persuade governments to provide protection against competition, or a budgetary subsidy. The essential quality of these activities is that, although they consume real resources and may well be highly profitable, they contribute nothing to output.[12] DUPs are thus seen as an *additional* cost of actual or potential policy interventions and a further reason, therefore, why an intervention in the face of a market failure may worsen rather than improve the situation. This theoretical insight has been particularly prominent in the literature on international trade policy.

Changing views on the efficiency effects of measures to reduce poverty and/or inequality have added to the growing scepticism about state interventions. This is chiefly an application of the point summarised in paragraph (d) above. In formal terms, in the absence of costless distortion-free taxes and subsidies, policies which redistribute incomes will necessitate departures from Pareto optimality[13] and thus create a trade-off between efficiency and

---

11. On this see Bhagwati, 1982; Bhagwati and Srinivasan, 1982; Krueger, 1974; and Tullock, 1980. Bhagwati and Srinivasan place DUPs into two categories: those triggered by policy actions and those seeking to influence policy. They may also be sub-divided into legal and illegal activities. Bhagwati gleefully points out that DUPs should be pronounced "dupes".

12. A qualification is necessary here, however, in that a DUP such as corruption can have the effect of alleviating the ill-effects of a distortion-creating intervention, e.g. by rendering it ineffective. It may then be associated with a higher level of output than would otherwise have occurred [Srinivasan, 1988 pp.556-7].

13. 'Pareto optimality', or Pareto efficiency, continues to occupy a role of enormous importance in micro theory and will recur at a number of points in this paper. It of course refers to a situation in which — for any given set of tastes, resources, technologies and distribution of incomes — it is not possible to change the allocation of resources without creating a situation in which it would pay the losers to bribe the gainers to return to the status quo ante. It requires, *inter alia*, the absence of scale economies and that marginal rates of transformation are everywhere equal to marginal rates of substitution. Frances Stewart points out to me that the trade-off referred to relates only to the secondary redistribution of income not to primary redistribution which seeks to narrow inequalities by enhancing the productive capabilities of the poor.

equality. Less formally, policy in the 1980s has been much concerned to improve economic incentives but the incentive problem is seen as the inverse of the income redistribution problem. This is an issue that is crystallised in debates about the desirable progressivity of income taxes.

Developments in the literature on market structures have also made a contribution to the retreat from interventionism, in the form of the theory of 'contestable' markets.[14] This introduces the idea that while there may not be competition *within* a given product market there may be competition *for* that market, and that the possibility of new entrants is itself a constraint on the exercise of monopoly power. The key condition is that the industry should be characterised by freedom of entry and exit. A firm can thus only be said to be a monopolist if it can discount the possibility of entry by a competitor. The relevance of this to the discussion in hand is that it apparently reduces the scope, or need, for state anti-monopoly measures. Even for 'natural' monopolies, the mere absence of actual competition within a market ceases to be an sufficient indicator of monopoly power.

These and other influences, in combination with the elaboration of the 'public choice' theory of government, help to explain a change of attitudes by many economists towards the nature of the state itself as an economic agent. Previously the general presumption was that the state was benign in its intentions, with the theory of policy centred around the question of how best the state could maximise social welfare.[15] There is nowadays far less readiness to assume that the state is benign, acting on behalf of the public interest to maximise social welfare.

Public choice theory, which has fruitfully applied the methods of economics to the analysis of politics, makes a contrary assumption: that the state as an institution, the government as a collectivity and politicians, bureaucrats and other individual actors in political processes each act to serve their own interests.[16] Within

---

14. On this see Baumol, Panzar and Willig, 1982 and 1985; and Baumol and Willig, 1987. Willig, 1987 pp.618-22, provides a useful short statement of the theory.
15. See, for example, Heal, 1973 p.59: "...the objective function in a planning problem serves to represent, or name numerically explicit, social preferences." See also Tinbergen, 1955, 1964 and 1967. This literature is discussed in the context of development planning in Killick, 1976.
16. For statements of public choice theory see Downs, 1957; Buchanan and Tullock, 1962; and Niskanen, 1971. See Bates, 1981, for an analysis in this tradition applied to agricultural marketing interventions in tropical Africa.

this model of politics the voter is analogous to the consumer in economic life, and democracy to consumers' sovereignty. The absence of democracy leads to maximisation of producers' [politicians, bureaucrats] surplus, rather than social welfare, and is thus analogous to monopoly.

The analogy is taken further in the literature on the 'predatory state'.[17] Thus, Lal sees the state as using its legal monopoly over the use of violence to maximise the 'profits' of government. He proposes a model of the state as a multiproduct natural monopoly, enjoying considerable scale economies in the production of its services of 'protection and justice'. He proceeds to apply the theory of contestable markets to suggest that the 'barriers to entry' — i.e. the factors which determine the probability that potential usurpers will emerge — will constrain the extent to which the state is able to use its powers in a predatory fashion, and to depart from promoting the interests of the populace. From this it is an easy step to suggest that openly competitive politics are beneficial to the interests of the general public. With special reference to developing country conditions, it has also been suggested that in predator-type situations, the state's appetite for revenues will tend to result in a closed-economy, import-substitution strategy, through taxes on trade and through an over-valuation of the currency resulting from use of the inflation tax.[18]

Other influences

A view of the state as an economic predator, exerting monopoly power to maximise its own revenues, was consistent with the seemingly inexorable rise during the 1960s and, especially, the 1970s in the size of the public sector relative to total economic

---

17. See especially Lal, 1984. Also Wellisz and Findlay, 1988.
18. Findlay, 1988; and Wellisz and Findlay, 1988. Note should also be made of a valuable analysis by Sandbrook [1986] of the ways in which the 'patrimonial' or personal rule systems of government which he sees existing in many African countries adversely affect economic performance. He sees this, and the personal loyalty and fear which underpin it, as highly destructive of capitalist development, through the pursuit of personal aggrandisement and short-term political advantage, and leading to economic irrationality. Political instability is endemic in this style of government, he believes, causing bureaucratic norms to give way to political and personal expediency, with the danger that abuse of office will become uncontrollable. Such states become less and less capable "of maintaining the political, legal and economic conditions that a flourishing capitalism requires. In extreme cases, the modern economy moves close to collapse." [p.328]. See also Jackson and Rosberg, 1984.

activity, as illustrated by the following statistics.[19] These show trends for all OECD countries taken together, expressed as percentages of GDP.

	total govt. expenditures	current govt. receipts
1960	28.5	28.3
1970	32.4	31.2
1980	39.3	35.7
1981	40.0	36.0
1982	41.4	36.1
1983	41.5	35.8
1984	40.5	35.6
1985	40.7	36.0
1986	40.2	35.7

Tax burdens were rising relative to incomes and the later-1970s saw the emergence of symptoms of a 'tax revolt' in various industrial countries. There was a growing belief, exacerbated by a slow-down in growth, that this trend could not continue indefinitely but that it would take a determined effort to halt the trend, let alone to reverse it. Such concerns, and doubts about the marginal benefits derived from additional expansions of state activity, contributed further to the shift in opinion away from interventionism. (In the event, it appears from these statistics that both expenditures and revenues (relative to GDP) peaked in the early 1980s, although the failure of either proportion to show much diminution since reinforces the view that actually reversing the trend will be a difficult task.)

This catalogue of influences on the retreat from *dirigisme* adds up to a rather formidable set of arguments. It has been derived, for the most part, from writers within the mainstream of economics. What should be added — and what makes the case all the stronger — is that the scepticism is by no means confined to those of a conservative disposition. Radical writers are scarcely less dismissive of interventionism. Perhaps representative of the radical viewpoint and writing from an apparently Marxian

---

19. From OECD *Economic Outlook*, December 1982 Tables R8 and R9, and June, 1988, Tables R14 and R15.

viewpoint, Dutkiewicz and Williams [1987 p.44] put it in terms that could as easily have come from the other end of the political spectrum: 'The "development states", in both the socialist and capitalist versions, have too often done little of what they could and should do, and too much of what they cannot or should not do, and much of that badly.' Or take Dearlove and White [1987, p.2], also writing from a socialist viewpoint: 'The case for the market and against the state is now widely accepted, not the least among socialist economists...' They might also have pointed to the economic reforms under way in China, the Soviet Union and other socialist countries which are based on a recognition that central planning approaches are not working well and a desire to make more, albeit carefully circumscribed, use of material incentives and market forces. Thus, in the Soviet Union the senior Politburo member responsible for ideology, Vadim Medvedev, is reported as saying that the marketplace is an 'irreplaceable means' of meeting consumer demand — a statement that would have been an unforgivable heresy a few years earlier.[20] We should also mention seemingly leftist governments in Western Europe, e.g. in France and Spain, which have undertaken policies more often associated with conservative governments;[21] and various other democratic socialist parties which have re-thought, or are attempting to re-think, their policies to make them less *dirigiste*, more accepting of market mechanisms.

It would not be correct to characterise this situation as a disillusionment, for Marxian writers have always viewed governments as representative of specific class interests, usually opposed to the interests of the mass of the population. They are inclined to agree with Adam Smith that, 'Civil government, so far as it is instituted for the security of property, is in reality instituted for the defence of the rich against the poor, or of those who have some property against those that have none at all.'[22] Radical writers thus have a good deal in common with more conservative authors in the public choice tradition in seeing the state as predatory rather than benign.[23] What to a less sceptical economist might look like

---

20. Quoted in *The Independent*, 6 October 1988.
21. See 'Editor's Introduction' to special issue on 'The Conservative Revolution' of *Economic Policy*, October 1987.
22. Quoted by Whynes and Bowles, 1981, p.36.
23. See Griffin and Gurley, 1985, for a valuable survey of the radical literature, with special reference to ldcs.

policy 'mistakes' may appear an entirely rational promotion of special interests to those — left or right — who see the state as acting on behalf of privileged interest groups.

In this account of the intellectual reasons for the retreat from *dirigisme* we should note finally the many resonances between changing attitudes in the industrial countries and the experiences of developing countries. This point scarcely needs elaboration. Suffice it to repeat what this author wrote on an earlier occasion on the lessons that 'have been established beyond reasonable dispute' from ldc experiences of the 1960s and 1970s:[24]

(i) Government actions are often not an expression of the general good. Frequently they are particularistic, promoting the interests of special groups: the armed forces; landowners and/or businessmen; the urban as against the rural population; and so on.

(ii) Medium-term development planning has in most ldcs almost entirely failed to deliver the advantages expected of it.

(iii) There are many instances of inefficiency and poor financial performance among the various kinds of parastatal enterprises and there are deep-seated reasons why this situation is likely to remain.

(iv) Many ldcs *did* over-emphasise industrialisation and neglect agriculture; and much of the industrialisation occurred with inadequate attention to efficiency and international competitiveness...

(vi)... many ldcs did themselves damage by an inward-looking approach to development, which failed to recognise the benefits to efficiency of remaining open to competition in world markets. They also over-valued exchange rates, which discouraged exports, encouraged import dependency and aggravated the foreign exchange constraint on development.

(vii) Other things being equal, people — as producers and consumers — *are* responsive to price incentives; relative prices are therefore important. It has aptly been remarked by Peter Timmer that 'Getting prices right is not the end of economic development, but getting prices wrong frequently is.'

24. From Killick, 1986 p.103. See the original for supporting evidence and references.

To sum up, it is evident that the intellectual strands brought out in this section are responses to genuine felt deficiencies, by no means just a matter of fashion or fad. There is no case for trying to turn back the clock and reverting to the approaches of earlier decades, nor would there be intellectual support for such a regression. But with any human response to a stimulus there is a danger of over-reaction, and there is evidence of a realisation of this in economics. It is to this that we turn next.

3
Rethinking the Role of the State

The partial rehabilitation of the state

First, by no means all the brave promise of post-Keynesian macro theorising to banish the state from the tasks of economic stabilisation has been fulfilled. There has, in fact, been a substantial decline in enthusiasm for monetarist, RE and NCM theory. The research from which Friedman derived many of his policy conclusions has been subjected to severe methodological criticism [Hendry and Ericsson, 1983] to which no response has been forthcoming. The monetarist approach to policy has also been undermined by large and rapid shifts in the demand-for-money function which the theory assumes to be stable [Judd and Scadding, 1982]. Private sector behaviour is not now regarded as stabilising in the way postulated by monetary theory and that theory is now seen as glossing over the large difficulties of defining and controlling money supply, given greater force as a result of recent innovations in financial instruments [Vines, 1986].

'Natural rate' theories of unemployment are also now being regarded with more scepticism. Such theories differentiate sharply between structural and cyclical unemployment but recent research indicates that the two in fact tend to move together, raising questions about whether they are separate, independent and identifiable components of total unemployment, as 'natural rate' theory requires.[25] In more polemical vein, Solow [1987 pp 182-83] has complained that, 'the way in which modern macroeconomists toss around the notion of a "natural rate of unemployment or employment" is a sort of intellectual scandal,' allowing them to describe as fully employed economies with high recorded

---

25. Haltiwanger [1987 pp.610-12] provides a concise statement of the present state of this literature.

unemployment. He cites an OECD study which shows that no explanatory value is lost if the 'natural rate' is substituted by a three-year average of past actual total unemployment rates.

There have been retreats too on the RE and NCM fronts. Rational expectations theory is particularly criticised for the unrealistic claims it makes for individuals' ability and willingness to absorb and process information, and to act upon the results. RE models assume that agents behave as if they know as much about the structure of the economy as the policy-makers, even though the structure and underlying relationships are constantly changing.[26] There are also criticisms of its logical consistency.[27] There are analogous criticisms of the extreme assumptions of the NCM approach, of its difficulty in explaining unemployment in a market-clearing context and its inability to explain observed real effects of monetary policy.[28]

Perhaps most pertinent to our present purposes, none of the successive attempts in the new macroeconomics to 'prove' the inevitable impotence of government attempts at macro management is regarded as having succeeded, mainly because of the extreme assumptions that have to be made for the proofs to hold. Thus, Friedman's 'proof' that active monetary policies will be entirely ineffective rests on *simultaneous* stabilising actions by the private sector [Maddock and Carter, 1982]. We have referred already to the extreme assumptions of the RE model; the NCM school is vulnerable to the same attack, not only because it takes over the assumptions of rational expectations theory but also because the NCM model is one in which all markets clear and instantaneously [thus making all unemployment voluntary]. Attempts by Barro [1974], McCallum [1980] and others to show the inevitable impotence of government policy because of completely

---

26. See Friedman, 1979, and Schiller, 1978 on the extreme informational assumptions of RE theory. Perry, 1984 p.406, cites work by Schultz which does not suggest that people react to, or anticipate, government actions in the ways that RE theory requires them to do.

27. Sargent, 1984 and 1987 p.78 explores this and explains it in the following terms 'There is a logical difficulty in using a rational expectations model to give advice... For suppose that the economist's advice is persuasive in the sense that it alters the probabilities attached to future government actions. Then the economist was not really using rational expectations equilibrium to interpret the historical observations, having attributed to agents expectations about government policy that did not properly take into account his advice.'

28. See Fischer, 1987 pp.647-51, for a survey of recent literature on the NCM approach.

offsetting behaviour by private agents [complete crowding out] are no longer regarded as successful, or even helpful. Models which modify the RE and NCM assumptions, while retaining many other features, suggest there is scope for active government macro management.[29] Indeed, by also drawing attention to the importance of the supply side in macroeconomic performance the new theories may actually point to the need for a wider range of policy interventions. Thus, Meade [1982] argues that many other policy instruments have to be combined with measures aimed at money wage stabilisation in order to reconcile that with low unemployment, including profit-sharing incentives, a wage inflation tax, employment subsidies, etc.

At a practical policy-making level there is also evidence of a retreat from the more *laissez faire* approaches of the earlier 1980s. Beckerman has pointed to the similarities between the 'New Cambridge' doctrines that were severely criticised by monetarist and RE writers a few years ago and the received wisdom of the present time that sees a strong link between the budgetary and balance of payments deficits of the USA; and to the apparent reversion to Keynesian orthodoxy in solutions advocated by the Group of Seven.[30] The recognition of the UK Chancellor of the Exchequer, in common with the finance ministers of the other G7 countries, of the costs of freely floating market-determined exchange rates, and their conversion to the merits of managed rates provides a further example. There has also been a substantial retreat from the prescriptions of strict monetarism, which have proved politically and technically unfeasible. Thus the conservative economist von Weizsacker [1987, p.192]:

> Experience of conservative macroeconomic policy in recent years has shown that a steady growth of money supply is politically not viable. The central banks had to allow an over-shoot of their monetary targets in order to avoid a recession, and that is what they did. The credibility of monetary targets was thereby substantially reduced.

None of the above should be read as implying that the new theories have been wholly rejected. Far from it. For instance, Benjamin Friedman's recommendation that government policies should be

---

29. Fischer, 1987, and Maddock and Carter, 1982.
30. Wilfred Beckerman, 'Fear spurs Keynesian converts', *The Independent*, 11 January 1988.

targeted to achieve some given and stable rate of growth of *nominal* GDP has become orthodoxy.[31] (This rule does seem curious, though, for neither governments nor their citizenry are likely to be indifferent about the shares of real growth and inflation in any increase in nominal GDP, in which case it might be better to have separate targets for each.) There is similar acceptance of the main thrust of the RE school: that policy-makers must in designing policies take the expectations of the public more fully into account, a requirement which considerably adds to the complexities of policy formation and which probably reduces the probability that a given policy will achieve the desired result. It is the more extreme anti-intervention claims of some advocates of the new theories which are rejected.

There is a similar story to tell when it comes to the policy implications of the theory of contestable markets. There has been developed a theory of perfectly contestable markets, analogous to perfect competition, from which a case can be derived for reduced state anti-monopoly interventions. Here too, however, extremely demanding conditions must be satisfied for a market to be perfectly contestable, including the complete absence of any legal, cost or other constraints on entry and exit from the market, including the absence of sunk costs. Only when these conditions are satisfied will 'hit and run' competition of the type that would constrain an incumbent monopolist be possible. Clearly such conditions are unlikely to be satisfied in the real world, particularly in 'natural monopoly' industries, so that the potential scope for anti-monopoly interventions is, in practice, not much reduced. What the theory does do, however, is to remind us of the importance of entry conditions in conditioning the scope for monopoly rents and as a variable for policy to influence.

In other areas too there are trends in the literature that reassert the potential value of government interventions, and which disagree with the view that most economic distortions are the result of such interventions. Thus, the concept of 'market failures' has proved quite robust against the criticisms of pro-market writers. Stiglitz, 1986 p.90, provides the following summary of eight chief, interrelated, types of market failure:

---

31. Thus, Vines, 1986 p.6, reports 'rather widespread support' for this, with its implication that inflation will not be passively accommodated.

(1) Failures of competition, existence of monopoly power.

(2) The existence of certain desirable goods and services that would not be supplied [or not efficiently] by private markets because they could not be made profitable — public goods.

(3) Externalities: disbenefits which are not reflected in producers' costs; benefits which are not reflected in their revenues.

(4) Incomplete markets, where markets fail to produce items which people desire even though they would be willing to pay more than the cost of production for them. Various kinds of insurance are a common example, as are forward markets. Also covered here is the case of inadequate co-ordination of complementary producers, a type of failure closely associated with Scitovsky [1954].

(5) Information failures, most notably a tendency to under-produce information to which access cannot be limited. Other examples include possible creation of *mis*information, necessitating regulations to secure truthfulness in advertising.

(6) Macroeconomic disequilibria, including inflation and cyclical unemployment.

(7) Poverty and inequality: market solutions may result in conditions which are inconsistent with societal preferences on such matters.

(8) Because individuals do not always act in what is regarded by the state as their own best interests, the need for governments to promote or produce 'merit goods'. Laws requiring seat belts to be worn in cars are an example; health warnings against cigarettes are a negative illustration.

In addition to these largely 'allocative' failures, there is also an important set of what has been described as *dynamic*, or 'creative', market failures. This refers to failures to expand the production frontier at an optimal rate. This might result, for example, from suboptimal levels of investment and innovation, perhaps due to scale economies, or from inadequate supplies of entrepreneurial abilities to exploit economic opportunities and propel the economy forward.[32]

---

32. See Arndt, 1988, building on Kaldor's ideas about the creative functions of the market mechanism, as "an instrument for transmitting impulses to economic change" [1972, p.1240].

Relatedly, there has in recent years been particular interest in the issues thrown up by various kinds of 'Prisoner's Dilemma' and by the existence of common property rights.[33] A 'new political economy' school has grown up which is principally interested in situations — such as those described by the Prisoner's Dilemma — in which co-operative solutions, which may conflict with the outcomes resulting from atomistic maximising behaviour, produce superior results. The conclusion of this set of writings is that co-operative behaviour cannot be secured voluntarily, leaving the state as a probable agency for enforcing a co-operative solution.[34]

Both in the literature and in politics, there has also been growing concern with environmental issues. In their economic aspects, these largely concern the existence of important external diseconomies — side-effects of industrial and agricultural production which are harmful to society but are not fully reflected in production costs and are thus over-produced. It has been stated that 'the theory of technological externalities is essentially the foundation of environmental economics' [Lafont, 1987 p.263] and that is a branch of economics that urges a wide range of policy interventions.

Mention was made earlier of the theory of directly unproductive profitseeking (DUP) activities as giving increasing weight to the costs of policy-induced economic distortions. Here too, however, the theory is not unambiguously anti-interventionist for many DUPs result from the existence of monopoly power, and the scarcity-premia which it can create, which can just as well occur in the private as the public sector.[35]

Finally, it should be said that debates about what the evidence shows concerning the relative efficiency of markets and state interventions are far from over. For example, the evidence comparing the performance of private and public enterprises is far from uniformly in favour of the former; and the chief conclusion of analyses of the policy of privatisation or divestiture is that the

---

33. See Rapoport, 1987, for a brief survey of this literature.
34. See Inman, 1985, for an account of this literature. Arrow's [1951 and 1987] impossibility theorem is an important contribution to this literature, showing that governments can either choose Pareto-efficient policies or be non-dictatorial, but not both.
35. See Tullock, 1987, who observes that "The activity of creating monopolies is a competitive industry" and who stresses the socially harmful effects of private sector rent-seeking efforts.

degree of competition in an industry is a more important determinant of the economic and social efficiency of an enterprise than the nature of its ownership.[36] And it has not gone unnoticed that two of the most successful economies of the post-war period — Japan and South Korea — are scarcely exemplars of the free-market model.

While there has, thus, been a partial rehabilitation in economics of the desirability of state interventions in the macroeconomic and microeconomic management of the economy, how extensive those interventions should be and what boundaries should be drawn round the role of the state remain the subjects of intense debate. The next section therefore explores some of the outstanding issues.

The role of the state: clarifications and complications

In considering the desirable role of the state there are essentially two different issues, which are sometimes confused: (a) *how large* should the state be in relation to total economic activity; and (b) *what types of policy instrument* should the state employ?[37] To ask, Is it likely to be in the public interest for the state to intervene here? is different from the question, If so, what would be the most effective type of measure for it to introduce?

A particularly common source of confusion is between arguments for a reduction in the role of the state and arguments for a shift from policies of planning and control to policies which work through markets. Suggestions, for example, for a change in government import policies from quantitative restrictions to tariffs are not, *per se*, about the extent to which government action is necessary to limit imports but about the most efficient way of achieving that objective. Similarly, the liberalisation of financial markets does not do away with the need for policy instruments to influence the volume of credit and may well be associated with the creation of new regulatory bodies to safeguard the interests of depositors and investors.

---

36. For comparisons of private and state-owned enterprise performance see Millward and Parker, 1983; Millward, 1988; and Yarrow, 1986. For broader examinations of the economics of divestiture see Kay and Thompson, 1986; and various contributions in Cook and Kirkpatrick [eds], 1988. See Hanke, 1987a and 1987b for statements of the economic case for privatisation.
37. The question, How Large, of course begs large questions about how this might be measured, for many of the ways in which the state impinges upon economic life are not amenable to quantification.

As has already been suggested, the balance of the arguments about 'controls versus markets', as they relate to policies in ldcs, has shifted against controls, with major implications for the design of policy strategies. While there is a tendency in that direction, shifting policies in more market-oriented directions is not synonymous with reducing the relative role of the state. For one thing, it is entirely open to governments to make the judgement that some prices are too important to be left to markets alone to determine [Williamson, 1985 p.47]. Interest, wage and exchange rates are obvious examples. At a more micro level, fuel and agricultural input prices are among those in which the government is likely to take a close interest, not to mention the prices charged by private monopolies. As Lamb [1987 p.15] has aptly put it: 'Market-oriented policy reforms [in ldcs] often in practice alter rather than reduce demands on public institutions — because intervention must compensate for widespread economic distortions, because efficient market functioning demand considerable sophistication in information and services to producers, or because there is a high degree of interconnection with other policy areas.'

The question of how large the state should be, asked generally, is often an unhelpful one. Ideological and other preferences and the policy objectives that arise from them, past practices, socio-economic structures, the supply of private entrepreneurship — as well as the capabilities of the state itself — are all factors which differ markedly between countries, which is why the relative importance of the public and private sectors varies so much across countries. Since the essence of the problem is one of balancing market failures against state failures, of calculating the costs of state inaction against the costs of state intervention, the solution which suggests itself is that the respective roles of the public and private sectors should be determined by the comparative advantage of each.[38] There are, of course, intractable measurement problems involved in such an application of a cost-benefit

---

38. Berry, 1987 p.210, provides a nice illustration of this way of looking at things:
'a useful null hypothesis in dealing with the economics of the labour market [in developing countries] is that very few direct policy interventions in the market are likely to have significantly beneficial effects after allowance is made for the fact that when undertaken they are unlikely to be carried out in an optimal fashion because of lack of information, lack of efficient policy instruments, political biases, or administrative incompetence and corruption.'

approach. Another difficulty is that evaluators' objectives differ, some placing more importance, say, on personal liberty, others on the satisfaction of basic wants. As a result, there would be disagreement about the 'shadow prices' that should be employed in such an evaluation. Nevertheless, the comparative advantage approach has merits as a way of thinking about this subject, particularly for those of a pragmatic bent.

Interestingly, a comparative advantage, case-by-case, approach is given specific theoretical backing from two directions. The first of these is derived from the 'problem of the second best'.[39] The upshot of this theoretical literature is that the proposition that there are no general policy solutions in a second-best world is a robust one but that it may be possible, in concrete instances, to work out second-best policies, following careful analysis of all the ramifications of alternative policies.[40]

Writings on Arrow's impossibility theorem, referred to earlier, arrive at a very similar destination from a different starting point. Given a trade-off between Pareto efficient policies and non-dictatorial governments, 'a preferred mix of market and governmental — voluntary and coercive — institutions requires a delicate balancing of pluses and minuses for neither institutional form clearly dominates the other' [Inman, 1985 p.739]. Not the least of the reasons for this 'delicate balancing' is that Arrow shows that a policy action is only unambiguously good [or bad] for society if all individuals are identical. We have no way of determining *a priori* what mix of private and public would result from calculations which attempt to strike balances between benefits and disbenefits, nor is it likely to be fruitful to search for one.[41]

Having made the basic point, it is, however, necessary to add some qualifications. First, while it is often over-stressed, the

---

39. Lipsey and Lancaster's [1956, p.11] classical statement of the problems of the second-best states:

'The general theory of the second best optimum states that if there is introduced into a general equilibrium system a constraint which prevents the attainment of one of the Paretian conditions, the other Paretian conditions, although still attainable, are, in general, no longer desirable.'

The implication of this is that in the face of the multiple infractions of Pareto optimality, and constraints on policy, that characterise the real world a given policy intended to correct one of these may actually lead to a net reduction in economic welfare, even though it appears to be moving the economy in the direction of Pareto optimality, thus seeming to call into question the basis for much policy advice. See McKee and West, 1981, for a recent survey.

40. See Bohm, 1987, for a brief review of the present state of this debate.

question of the absolute size of the state *is* significant in terms of its implications for liberty (see below page 37) and for the incentive effects of the resulting levels of taxation and state provision. Since many interventions are revenue-using they imply greater taxation and since neutral taxes are unavailable this taxation thus tends to have adverse effects on economic incentives that must be set against any positive effects that may result from the interventions themselves.

Second, we should note that the clear distinction we have so far been drawing between the public and private sectors is in practice often absent, particularly in ldcs. This is clearly the case in the productive system where between the 'pure' cases of public and private enterprises there are likely to be jointly-owned ventures, public concerns with hired-in private sector managements, private concerns operating publicly-licensed franchises, co-operatives, and so on. In the use of resources too, the distinction between public and private consumption may be blurred, for example, through the use of public subsidies for basic necessities, or 'privately-provided' education, health and housing.

The more general — and important — point, however, is that state-private relationships are generally symbiotic. The returns to a new factory, for example, may depend crucially on investment by the state in a new road — and the economic viability of that road may depend no less crucially on its use by the factory. In terms of personnel, too, it can be hard to know private from public agents, as in governments and public administrations many of whose members are actively engaged in business; or where private agents are so beholden to the state for their incomes as to effectively eliminate their independence. A further illustration is in the realm of taxation, where government revenues from a given tax system are highly sensitive to the level of activity in the private

---

41. It could be objected that the sharp distinction drawn here between the How much? and What kind? questions is invalid because it is not sensible to try to answer the former without some idea of what instruments are available to the state and their likely effectiveness. While it might be regarded as desirable in principle, say, that the state should intervene in the presence of private monopoly power, if the costs of feasible anti-monopoly measures could be shown to exceed the likely benefits then that would modify the desirability of intervention *per se*. While a valid argument, note that it is one that is automatically handled within a cost-benefit framework, since it is the expected net benefits or disbenefits of specific policy instruments that would be included in the judgement. The resulting scale of state actions would thus be a function of the expected effectiveness of its policies.

sector, just as the performance of the private sector will be influenced by the structure of the tax system. It is also possible that the abandonment by the state of a policy that was having adverse economic effects would strengthen its capacities to act effectively elsewhere in the economy, for example, by permitting it to concentrate its resources on a narrower range of tasks, or by raising its credibility with the general public.[42] To return to the examples of Japan and South Korea, the lesson to be learned from their success is *not* that they left markets free — for they did not — but that in both cases the relationships established between their governments and private sectors were highly supportive, non-antagonistic.

A closely related difficulty about delineating the desirable role of the state concerns the fuller appreciation economists now have of the complex interrelations that commonly exist between a policy intervention and the economic system. It was, for example, growing understanding of the complex interactions between target and instrument variables that contributed to the erosion of Keynesian orthodoxy and awareness that well-intended policies could easily be dysfunctional, especially when time lags were introduced (see page 10 above).[43]

The recent literature on fiscal stance and on the economic effects of budgetary deficits is similarly much concerned with the feedbacks between fiscal and other economic variables, since much of government revenue and some expenditures are partially determined by the level of economic activity as a whole — a factor which makes it difficult to ensure that fiscal policy moves the economy in the way intended. For related reasons the concept of the 'structural' budget deficit is employed, which relates to the deficit that would result from a given set of fiscal decisions *and* some trend value of GDP. Indeed, Buiter [1985, p.54] goes so far as to say that, 'there are no "model-free" measures of fiscal impact

---

42. Writing about the position in African countries, Booth, 1987, envisages a situation in which liberalisation and withdrawal by the state so enhances the development of civil society as to subsequently increase the state's ability to realise given objectives.
43. See Vines, 1986, who goes on to draw attention to the value of optimal control theory as a technique for tracing feedbacks and identifying trade-offs. See also Kendrick, 1988, on this. It is also interesting that, approaching the matter from a structuralist viewpoint, Chenery, 1988 p.61, also notes a movement towards a general-equilibrium approach to policy because of the complexities created by the manifold linkages between the different sectors of production.

on aggregate demand. Different views on how the economy works will give rise to conclusions about the demand effect of fiscal policy measures...that may differ not only in magnitude but even in direction.'

A second example of feedbacks can be drawn from recent writings on trade policy in conditions of imperfect competition. This draws attention to the dependence of the effects of trade policies on the precise nature of the structure of the industry in question. Thus, even though familiar principles of trade policy apply, no universal prescriptions emerge and "there is therefore a serious question about the government's ability to identify and implement desirable policy interventions" [Venables and Smith, 1986 p.638].

*   *   *

The argument thus far can be summarised as follows. Intellectual developments in the 1970s and 1980s raising questions about the effectiveness and desirability of state interventions in various aspects of economic life were a fruitful response to real problems. There is no question of reverting to the *status quo ante*. At the same time, there was a tendency for the reaction against *dirigisme* to go too far, with the more extreme theoretical attempts to 'prove' the impossibility of effective government action having been unsuccessful. There has thus occurred a partial rehabilitation of the state — but one which has left much scope for debate about the desirable extent of its involvement in the economy.

In approaching this question a comparative advantage approach can be useful, at least when there is a consensus about goals, leaving the resulting relative importance of public and private sectors to be determined as an outcome of the relative efficiencies of each sector. In any case, the dividing line between the 'public' and 'private' sectors is often cloudy. It has been suggested that there is increased support for the view that policies that operate through market forces are more likely to succeed than policies of control and command. The effect of this is likely to limit the scope for state interventions to some extent; greater awareness of the complexity of policy-economy interactions also provides a reason for caution in urging policy interventions.

The next two chapters are about the extent to which it is legitimate and helpful to apply to developing countries the conclusions of modern *mainstream* normative theory.[44] The next chapter argues the need for caution but Chapter 5 then draws attention to specific areas where such applications may well be fruitful.

---

44. 'Mainstream' is largely used in this paper to refer to the neoclassical school but the term is sometimes extended to cover other parts of orthodox, or received, theory. By 'neoclassical' is meant marginalist theory based upon methodological individualism.

4
The Case for Caution and Modesty

Much of what has happened to development economics in recent years, and to economists' policy advice to the governments of ldcs, is directly linked to the changes that have been occurring in mainstream economics. The need for care is argued below, however, on the grounds (a) that mainstream economics contains value biases which are not necessarily appropriate for application to ldcs; (b) that important areas of mainstream economics are, in any case, in a highly unsettled state; (c) that the relevance of many of the policy positions of the dominant neoclassical school is particularly open to question; and (d) that, even at the level of theory, mainstream economics contains contextual and institutional biases towards conditions in advanced economies, which also reduces the transferability of its conclusions.

Value biases

Some economists have aspired to develop a body of theory which is value free and have thus drawn a sharp distinction between positive and normative economics, with positive economics offering 'objective or scientific explanations of the working of the economy.'[45] Its normative, policy recommendations can thus be presented as based upon a 'scientific' body of knowledge which is itself value-free. Economists urging this position have adopted a logical positivism which, however, is now widely rejected by philosophers, among other reasons, for being too crude in the relationship it postulates between 'facts' and values.[46] The nature

---

45. The definition is from the popular textbook by Begg, Fischer and Dornbusch [1987, p.13].
46. See Walsh, 1987, on which this paragraph is based. See also Caldwell, 1984, for a recent collection of readings; and Toulmin, 1950, for a fascinating study of the role of reason in ethics.

of the difficulty is well illustrated by the way economists use 'optimum' as a technical expression, as in 'Pareto optimum'. Is it not inevitable that what 'scientific explanations' conclude to be optimal will come also to be regarded as 'good'? Pareto optimality, after all, is a condition of equilibrium (itself a loaded word: equilibrium = desirable; disequilibrium = uncomfortable) in which *welfare* is maximised.[47] It is, however, a particular kind of welfare, as is argued below, and one based upon atomistic self-interested decisions. Major bodies of 'positive' theory — of competition, of the working of the macroeconomy, of international trade — so intimately impinge upon human well-being that it is impossible to retain an ethical neutrality about their constituent parts. This helps to explain the passion with which apparently technical disagreements are often argued.

The pretentiousness of positivistic claims for economics is further revealed when we consider the nature of Pareto optimality. First, this is based upon individual rationality — the consistent pursuit of self-welfare.[48] This creates difficulties in situations where co-operative solutions would produce unambiguously better results than outcomes based upon atomistic rationality — the type of problem addressed in the literature on the Prisoner's Dilemma and the Tragedy of the Commons.[49] In the latter instance, for example, while it would be in the collective interests of all cattle-owners having access to communal grazing grounds to introduce measures safeguarding against over-grazing, individually each of them has an interest in making the fullest possible use of his right of access. Given its grounding in individualistic rationality, it is perhaps inevitable that mainstream economics tends to neglect state interventions that promote social rationality.

---

47. See note 13 on Pareto optimality. Other loaded words may also be cited. Note, for example, the use of 'intervention' to describe a policy action by the state, implying laissez faire as a 'normal' condition. There is also the amusing case of 'the Leontief paradox'. This was the result of an application of the Hekscher-Ohlin theory of international trade to the pattern of trade of the USA. That this test appeared to produce results which were inconsistent with the received comparative advantage theory was called a paradox rather than a refutation.

48. This is not the same as selfishness, however, for individuals may incorporate a desire for the welfare of others in their own preferences, but the facts of altruism and what Sen has called 'commitment' are difficult to handle within the framework of individual rationality. See Sen, 1985A and B, and also his 1988 Marshall lectures on 'Social rationality' [forthcoming].

49. See footnote 33.

Related to this is the implicit view which mainstream economics takes of the nature of liberty. There is a long-standing (and still unresolved) philosophical debate between those who (like mainstream economists) view liberty as a negative condition — the absence of coercion, or *laissez faire* — and those who espouse a positive view of liberty — relating it to a person's ability to realise his own goals and implying in economic life some minimal access to 'basic needs'.[50] This is a particularly important distinction in the conditions of low-income countries, where many cannot afford even basic necessities.

It is not difficult to relate this identification of mainstream economics with a negative view of liberty to political conservatism; and the same connection can be made to its lack of interest in the distribution of income and wealth. Distributional outcomes are not included in the economist's definition of efficiency, and there is a Pareto-efficient allocation of resources for each different income distribution. In many eyes, this seriously reduces the weight that should be attached to the objective of securing Pareto-efficiency because, as Stewart has put it [1985, p.286], 'If any given income distribution is considered to be wrong then maximising on that basis may lead to a worse outcome than taking a Pareto-inferior decision that leads to a better income distribution.'

More generally, there is an evident affinity between the 'conservative revolution' in economic policy which is under way in major industrial countries and the neoclassical renaissance which has occurred in economics in recent years. This 'revolution' has been described in the following terms:[51]

* A perception that the trade-off between efficiency and equality was larger than had previously been thought.

* A growing feeling that the mere existence of a market failure did not mean that the government could do better.

* A judgement that inflation is more disruptive (and that unemployment is less disruptive) than was previously thought.

* A recognition that a series of short-term expedients does not cumulate to a satisfactory outcome in the longer run.

---

50. See Berlin, 1969, for a classical discussion of these two approaches, and Dasgupta, 1986, for an application of it to contemporary trends in economic policy.
51. See the special issue of *Economic Policy*, October 1987, on the Conservative Revolution. My list is culled from the summaries offered there by the editors and George Yarrow [pp.13, 198-99].

To which, in more jaundiced vein, Solow has added [1987, pp.182-83]:

   * A desire to redistribute income from the poor to the rich.

The connections between this and trends in economics are clear: the reassertion of the superiority of market allocations; rejection of Keynesian approaches and attempts to substitute monetarist solutions; a shift from distributional to efficiency priorities; and from a positive to a negative view of liberty. We should note, however, that the conservative revolution has involved a far from pure application of market principles; witness the growth in protectionism in the same period.

The relevance of the above suggestions of value biases in mainstream economics to the theme of this monograph is that the issues of positive versus negative liberty, of allocative efficiency versus distributional objectives and, perhaps, of individual versus social welfare arise more intensely, are closer to centre stage, in poorer countries. Indeed, the chief thrust of new writings on development in the later-1960s and earlier 1970s was to emphasise the inadequacy of passive, or trickle-down, approaches to poverty alleviation and the importance of incorporating distributional, or basic needs, goals in development strategies of 'redistribution through growth'.[52] And just as it was said earlier that there can be no going back to the *dirigisme* of earlier times so, hopefully, there can be no return to trickle-down. There is also the political aspect. While it was related to developments in economics, the conservative revolution was the result primarily of changes in public attitudes, who expressed these changes by electing more conservative governments. There is little evidence, however, of a parallel *general* shift to conservatism among developing countries, so that policy prescriptions which sit well in some industrial countries may be inconsistent with social objectives in many developing countries.

Divisions in economics

In addition to its value biases, the existence of major divisions within mainstream economics is another reason for exercising care

---

52. See Chenery et al, 1974, for the classic statement of this position. See Cornia et al, 1987, for a recent contribution in this tradition, relating to the design of adjustment policies in developing countries.

in exporting its conclusions for application in developing countries. Quite apart from Marxian and other radical critiques, there are writers who have far more in common with the prevailing orthodoxy in microeconomics but who nonetheless are serious critics of it. We will later examine other criticisms of the neoclassical school and so will confine ourselves here to mentioning the major tension between neoclassicism and more behavioural approaches to economic life. Neoclassical economics is a behavioural 'black box', proceeding by assumption and often explicitly rejecting the validity of those who would 'enquire within' into actual behaviour.[53] Against the standard neoclassical assumptions, that people have well defined preference functions, will make consistent choices in pursuit of these preferences, and will choose that set of available transactions which will maximise their welfare, behaviouralists perceive a more limited type of rationality, what Simon has called 'bounded' rationality.[54] He argues that, in practice, people adopt decision strategies designed to cope with the many limitations on the information the individuals can acquire and relate to their objectives. These give rise to behaviour patterns which differ from those postulated by neoclassicists.

Simon and others have expressed doubt about the appropriateness of optimisation as the key to economic behaviour, with 'satisficing' suggested as a more realistic model. Nelson and Winter similarly stress the over-simplification involved in trying to understand the behaviour of firms in terms of maximisation, are critical of neoclassical disinterest in the firm as an economic institution and of its preoccupation with equilibrium models, arguing that standard micro theory has not been good at coping with the diversity of firm characteristics and the way this interacts with industry structures.[55]

The purpose of introducing these considerations here is not to necessarily agree with the critics but to urge that their work has to be taken seriously [as it is] and that it draws attention to some

---

53. This is under the influence of Milton Friedman's 'as if' approach, that it does not matter that a theory makes unrealistic behavioural assumptions so long as market outcomes are 'as if' economic agents behave as the models postulate.

54. See Simon, 1982; also Oliver Williamson, 1985.

55. Nelson and Winter, 1982, passim. Leibenstein, 1966 and 1987, is also critical of the neoclassical behavioural assumptions and presents a theory of 'X-efficiency' as coping better with observed behavioural facts. Various other writers have presented models which see the firms' decisions as the outcome of the interactions of coalitions of interests within it, or as maximising goals other than profits.

of the limitations of neoclassical theory. Appearances of a consensus notwithstanding, microeconomics is seriously divided and that is a situation which should condition the confidence with which *any* school presents its policy recommendations.

If microeconomics is divided, macroeconomics is close to anarchy. In an authoritative recent survey of trends in macroeconomics Fischer [1988 p.331], for example, has written of 'remarkable progress in understanding many theoretical issues...' but '...confusion at the business end of macroeconomics, in understanding the actual causes of macroeconomic fluctuations, and in applying macroeconomics to policy-making.' In elucidating the differences in this branch of economics, we can do no better than follow the account offered by Begg et al, [1987, chapter 30]. They see disagreements among macroeconomic theorists as centred around three issues: (a) the speed with which markets clear, particularly the labour market; (b) the way in which expectations are formed; and (c) the relative importance of the short- and long-run. They further classify macro theorists into four groups, although some arbitrariness is inevitable here:

(i) **The 'new classical macroeconomists'.** These assume that the labour market clears almost instantaneously, with fully flexible prices and wages. They therefore deny the significance of the short-run/long-run distinction; and they adopt the rational expectations model, with its strong informational and behavioural assumptions.

(ii) **The gradual monetarists.** These take a less sanguine view of the speed with which the labour market clears, believing it may take a few years. They thus accept that short-run macroeconomic behaviour differs from the long run but urge that the long run should be given precedence. No uniform view is taken on the formation of expectations, except to stress the policy-neutralising effects when people come to anticipate government policies.

(iii) **Eclectic Keynesians,** who are described as "short-run Keynesians and long-run monetarists." They think that it takes a substantial time for the labour market to achieve equilibrium and, therefore, that the management of aggregate demand is important during the transitional phase. They are inclined to think that expectations respond only sluggishly.

(iv) **Extreme Keynesians,** identified with the Cambridge school.

These think that labour markets clear only very slowly, if ever, with real wages sticky in the downward direction, and that expectations also adjust only slowly. Thus, the 'short run' may last a long time and demand management policies are of great importance and potency.

Table 1 reproduces Begg *et al's* stylised summary of these opposing schools.

Table 1
A Stylized Picture of the Competing Macroeconomic Views

	New Classical	Gradualist Monetarist	Eclectic Keynesian	Extreme Keynesian
Market clearing	Very fast	Quite fast	Quite slow	Very slow
Expectations	Rational adjust quickly	Adjust more slowly	Could be fast or slow to adust	Adjust slowly
Long run/ short run	Not much difference since fast adjustment	Long run more important	Don't neglect short run	Short run very important
Full employment	Always close	Never too far away	Could be far away	Could stay far away
Policy conclusion	Demand management useless; supply side vital	Supply side more important but avoid wild swings in demand	Demand management important too	Demand management what counts

Source: Begg *et al*, 1987, p.679

Clearly, then, this literature is in a highly unsettled state, with some writing of a 'profound crisis' in macroeconomic theory [Vines, 1986]. Here again the point is not to take sides in the debate but rather to draw attention to the inappropriateness of making strong policy prescriptions, for developed and developing countries alike, from a body of theory in such turmoil.

International economics, which is of great importance to developing countries, is perhaps in better shape. As is suggested later, the 'new trade theory' has not made any major dents in the comparative advantage approach and has strengthened it in some respects. Overall, however, economic theory is in a very pluralistic phase, and this is a reason for caution and modesty in urging it upon ldcs.

The costs of neoclassical dominance

While economics is in a pluralistic condition and received wisdoms are coming under more scrutiny, the neoclassical paradigm remains easily the most influential, at least in microeconomics and trade theory. That paradigm teaches that efficiency losses are to be expected from the dominance of a large firm in an industry, and it is arguable that economics too is suffering efficiency losses from neoclassical 'large firm' dominance. These mainly relate to the narrowness of its approach and the levels of abstraction which its analysis commonly incorporates. Hicks is not alone in suggesting that 'There is much of economic theory which is pursued for no better reason than its intellectual attraction; it is a good game.'[56]

One aspect of narrowness concerns the way in which neoclassical preoccupation with [allocative] Pareto efficiency, and its grounding in methodological individualism,[57] gets in the way of an adequate treatment of policy-making processes and thus reduces its normative usefulness. Reference was made earlier [p.15] to views of the state as benign or predatory. What both of these apparently opposite views incorporate, however, is a view of the state as an optimising entity, seeking to maximise the welfare either of the people as a whole or of some special interest groups. In this respect it takes over a key methodological feature of neoclassicism, explicitly so in the case of public choice theory.

Within such a framework there is no room for a more realistic view which is dubious about treating the state as an entity and sees governments as coalitions of competing interests, often

---

56. Hicks, 1979, p.viii, cited by Rashid, 1988, p.207. See also Colander and Klamer's [1987] survey of student perceptions, indicating mixed views on the relevance of neoclassical economics but a strong consensus that what matters for success as a student of economics is 'Being smart in the sense of being good at problem-solving' and 'Excellence in mathematics'; and that what matters least for this purpose is 'Having a broad knowledge of the economics literature' and — considered of easily the least importance — 'Having a thorough knowledge of the economy.'

57. By this is meant a methodology which takes individuals' pursuit of their own welfare as the motivating force of economic life, a pursuit which is to be reconciled with social welfare through the 'hidden hand' of the market.

preoccupied with the compromises of conflict management, in which policy decisions are the 'resultants' of bargaining between individuals, groups and agencies. As one political scientist has put it, 'There is every evidence that in complex policy situations, so-called decision makers do not strive to optimise some value nor is the notion of optimisation a useful way of ordering and analysing their behaviour regardless of their intentions.'[58] It similarly seems to reject the possibility of the state as 'soft', where power is widely diffused and policies are often not implemented as intended, or not enforced. The individualistic orientation of the theory does not allow it adequately to explain the organisation of society or its institutions, nor does it have room for power as an independent variable.[59] Further and characteristically, neoclassical approaches can be criticised as too static, not coping well with the dynamics of policy change.[60] Finally, the neoclassical disinterest in income distribution, noted earlier, is a further source of difficulty because the politics of economic policy-making are very largely about who will gain and who will lose.[61]

It might be retorted that economists are good at economics and it is not reasonable to expect them also to produce fully satisfactory models of politics. There would be more weight to that point, however, if they were more reticent in their willingness to propose policy 'reforms', and if it were not for the fact that in an earlier period, when the discipline was less preoccupied with formal modelling, economics had more to say about political processes.

One of the costs of the high level of abstraction of much contemporary theorising is that its normative conclusions often seem remote from realities. To take the example of trade policy,

---

58. Bauer, 1968, p.2. On policy decisions as resultants see Allison, 1971; see also Killick, 1976, for fuller discussion of these issues, as they relate to development planning. Corden, 1987 p.178, criticises public choice theory along similar lines. Sandbrook's illuminating view of the state in tropical Africa, summarised in footnote 18, illustrates the limitations of an optimisation framework, for his model is one in which the dynamics of political realities lead to 'irrational' economic results. It is not that he explicitly rejects an optimising framework but rather that to adopt such a framework would have been an obstacle to developing his considerable insights.
59. For criticisms along these lines see Dearlove, 1987, and Moore, 1987.
60. Toye, 1987 chapt. 5, develops arguments along these lines. He is mainly concerned to draw attention to the limitations of neo-Marxian views of the state but, as suggested earlier, there are strong affinities with this view and with those who see the state as predatory from a neoclassical viewpoint.
61. See Alt and Chrystal, 1983, p.248.

even though there is a consensus in the discipline in favour of the comparative advantage approach, the free trade thrust of its policy conclusions, being formally based on a wide range of demanding assumptions and relating mainly to static efficiency, seems often remote from the objectives or preoccupations of those responsible for trade policy.[62] To put the matter another way, while economists usually treat policy variables as exogenous, presumably for determination by government, political-economy approaches are more inclined to see policies as endogenously determined by competing pressures within the socio-economic system.[63]

Quite apart from its abstraction from important political realities, there are further grounds for questioning whether neoclassical theory provides a satisfactory basis for policy recommendations. The theory of policy interventions starts from the concept of market failures [see page 25] which relate to various ways in which actual economic conditions may depart from Pareto optimality. More recently, the notion of 'distortions' has come increasingly into use,[64] defined as deviations of relative prices from what would obtain in a perfectly competitive economy [Lal, 1983 p.111]. The emphasis here is on departures from optimality caused by government interventions, either as the principal result of a policy or as a by-product.

It is worth reminding ourselves at this point of some of the conditions that must be satisfied for perfect competition and Pareto optimality to exist. These include, for a perfectly competitive market: that all buyers and sellers are unable to influence the price they pay or receive; perfect information about available alternatives; complete freedom of entry and exit, including the absence of scale economies; complete homogeneity or standardisation of products, i.e. the absence of product

---

62. See Venables and Smith, 1986, who note that it seems to be widely accepted that governments ought to support dying, uncompetitive industries, the largely free-trade urging of economists notwithstanding.

63. In suggesting priorities for future research in development economics Ranis and Fei, 1988, see an increasing need to explain policies endogenously, as a function of initial conditions, and of interactions between economic performance and the institutional and policy setting. See also Baldwin, 1984, for an account of political-economy literature which seeks to explain the prevalence of protection and variations in levels of protection between industries. See also Corden, 1984a, for a discussion of the uses of mainstream freer trade policy recommendations in the light of the political-economy analyses.

64. The work of Corden, 1974, is particularly associated with this concept, although he traces it back to Meade, 1955.

differentiation; complete mobility of resources. For Pareto efficiency to exist, the conditions of perfect competition must be satisfied for *all* markets, including factor markets. If, in the interests of greater realism, the assumption of perfect information is dropped and uncertainty is introduced, then a complete set of contingent markets is necessary for Pareto efficiency to exist, in the enormously strong sense of there being a price for every commodity according to its physical attributes, its location, the dates upon which it will be produced or sold (i.e. complete forward markets), and the circumstances in which it will be sold.[65]

Pareto efficiency, in other words, is an idealised theoretical construct. As such, it has proved very valuable. But the question for us here is whether deviations from this condition can tell us anything about desirable policies in the real world, particularly in developing-country conditions. How, for example, could we substantiate a statement like, 'Most of the more serious distortions in the current workings of the price mechanism in third world countries are due not to the inherent imperfections of the market mechanism but to irrational government interventions...' [Lal, 1983 p.77]. Pareto efficiency does not appear to offer us a workable norm by which to judge real-world conditions because the basic nature of modern economic life imposes manifold departures from it which are, to a large extent, inescapable. Chenery [1975 p.315] has put the point well:

> ...it will never be possible to achieve perfect knowledge of instantaneous adjustment to market signals. It is therefore necessary to incorporate these 'imperfections' into the model itself. Once this has been done, it will become possible to take account of the existence of internal or external disequilibria and to devise more realistic policies to cope with them. In the theoretical literature, these policies are loosely referred to as 'second best' in relation to the neoclassical model. It would be more accurate to characterise the model itself as overly simple and 'first best' policies as simply unattainable.

It is this type of reasoning which has led behavioural economists to try to define some concept of 'workable competition' by which to judge actual market structures, rather than employ the unhelpfully idealised standard of perfect competition [Clark, 1940].

---

65. See Arrow, 1971 chapt. 4, on the necessity for complete markets in the presence of uncertainty.

Indeed, the theory of perfect competition turns out to be a double-edged weapon in debates about the superiority of market solutions, for it positively invites the conclusion that competition is inevitably imperfect [Helm, 1986 p.vii]. It is also likely to colour in undesirable ways the way we think about policy issues. Helleiner [1981, p.542] has put the argument eloquently in regard to the application of neoclassical theory to trade policy issues in ldcs, suggesting that it:

> accustoms the analyst to treating important elements of reality, such as oligopoly, transnational corporate intra-firm trade, or imperfect and asymmetrically available information, as mere 'wrinkles' on the 'general case'... the habits of thought develop which generate simple and almost subconscious and automatic, approaches to economic issues which... are far more complex than the core model would suggest. Almost imperceptibly, prisoners of their own paradigm, students of economics risk beginning to regard all government policies as 'interventions', likely to impede the harmonious functioning of markets; and to regard the distribution of income (and power) as a matter wholly independent of the market functioning, to be handled by separate policies (lump-sum transfers) which do not 'interfere' with markets.

We may regret also the limitations imposed by the static, or comparative-static, nature of most neoclassical analyses, and by their preoccupation with the properties of equilibrium. This has taught us much about the nature of competitive equilibrium but left us less well equipped to deal with dynamic processes or to understand what happens out of equilibrium. These are serious limitations, not the least when considering less-developed economies, and again undermine the foundations of neoclassical normative economics.[66] Various illustrations can be offered.

First, consider the lamentable state of growth theory, which sounds as if it ought to be of particular interest to students of development. Unfortunately this, in particular, suffers from the high level of abstraction referred to earlier, it being chiefly concerned with the *equilibrium* of a competitive economy over time, or with steady-state growth. As such, it is little addressed to the

---

66. See Fisher, 1983; also Scarf, 1960. Fisher argues that because mainstream theory does not offer much account of what happens out of equilibrium we have no rigorous basis for believing that equilibrium can be achieved, or sustained if disturbed.

lessons of history, to growth as a *process* and to such factors as entrepreneurship which are surely among the mainsprings of growth, not the least because they do not readily lend themselves to the methods of mathematical formalism which so dominate this branch of economics.[67] As one of the most distinguished growth theorists has put it [Solow, 1988 p.311]: 'Growth theory was invented to provide a systematic way to talk about and to compare equilibrium paths for the economy. In that task it succeeded reasonably well. In doing so, however, it failed to come to grips adequately with an equally important and interesting problem: the right way to deal with deviations from equilibrium growth.' In its present condition it is unclear how much of growth theory might be applied to any part of the real world but it is all too clear that it has little or no contact with the problems of ldcs. Thus the contents page of Sir John Hicks' *Capital and Growth* [1965] begins: '1. What is growth theory? 2. Nothing to do with "underdeveloped countries"'. In consequence, a subject of great importance has become a neglected aspect of economics[68], less fruitful to students of development than the growth accounting literature, for all the latter's absence of a strong theoretical basis.[69]

We may take as a second illustration the literature on the relationship between industry structure and technical progress. There could be little dispute that an understanding of the factors influencing the rate of technical progress and its spread at the enterprise level is of the most fundamental concern for long-term development. Unfortunately, however, the competitive-equilibrium framework of neoclassical theory does not facilitate exploration of such issues and it has largely been left to the Austrian school, working outside that framework, to pursue this matter.[70] Moreover, their hypothesis is one severely at odds with the pro-competition thrust of neoclassicism, i.e. that monopoly power favours innovation. The evidence does not wholly support either a pro-monopoly or a pro-competition stance, for it seems

---

67. See Rashid, 1988, for a fascinating discussion of this and other limitations imposed by the dominance of mathematical methods in economic theorising.
68. See the bibliography in Hahn, 1987, which contains just two references after 1970. However, see also Solow, 1988, for a few more recent references and a more positive view of the state of the subject.
69. See Maddison, 1987, for a recent survey of this literature.
70. See Schumpeter, 1961. See also Nelson and Winter, 1982, for an important critique of neoclassical theory from a broadly Schumpeterian viewpoint.

that market structures intermediate between the monopolistic and competitive extremes have the most intense pace of innovation, although innovation itself influences market structure.[71] The main point here, however, is that the neoclassical framework has little room for this important type of question.

As a final illustration of the neoclassical approach, a similar point might be made about the theory of international trade. We referred earlier to the strong support within the profession for Hekscher-Ohlin comparative advantage theories of trade but also to its remoteness from the concerns of policy-makers. There has hence remained much resistance to this theory within ldcs, partly because such a static approach seems to have limited relevance to the more dynamic questions about relationships between trade and development. Here too, the influence of trade on the rate and spread of technical progress is a key question — but not one that can easily be dealt with within a static comparative advantage framework. Rodrik [1988, p. 27] has recently argued that 'We are far from having any systematic theories which link trade policy to technical efficiency. In particular, we do not have any good reason to expect that trade liberalisation will generally be helpful to overall technological performance.' It is *possible*, particularly in large economies, that protection may foster innovation and long-run development: '...when all the complexities of real economies — differential rates of technical progress among industries, variable returns to scale and different income elasticities of demand for individual commodities — are considered, it can be argued that the analysis of the effects of trade and its normative implications may be considerably altered in a dynamic context.'[72] Again, the point is not to urge a pro-protectionist view but to point to the limitations of the neoclassical approach.

---

71. Kamien and Schwartz, 1982, conclude that, "Markets affording some opportunity for realising monopoly profits through invention, and in which incumbent firms' profits are vulnerable to erosion through innovation by others, appear to be the ones with the greatest level of innovative activity" but add that our present knowledge "is inadequate to allow for sweeping generalisations or universal formulas" [p.217]. See also Kamien, 1987.
72. Ros, 1987, p.577. See also Greenaway and Milner, 1987, and Stewart, 1984.

Contextual biases

Some of the points made earlier can be re-stated as drawing attention to what Seers as long ago as 1963 described as 'the limitations of the special case': the contextual bias in mainstream economic theory towards the economic structures and problems of advanced industrial economies. It is rare for even the most 'pure' theory to be free of such bias.[73] Thus, if we return to neoclassical micro theory, it is difficult to believe that the profession would have developed this in the ways that it has were most of its members living in low income countries. In such a situation they would surely have been less concerned with maximising the efficiency with which existing resources were utilised and more with how to increase those resources; less with getting onto the production possibility curve, more with shifting it outward. It is equally unlikely that growth theory would have been allowed to languish so, or that it would have centred around the qualities of steady-state growth.

Modern macroeconomic theory has a similar, but more overt, contextual bias. Much of present-day macro theory is concerned with how the markets for labour and capital work, and about information flows [see pp.40-41 above]. The operation of these markets will vary from economy to economy and questions like, do labour markets clear instantaneously or do economic agents have access to as much information about the economy as the government are less relevant in many developing-country contexts. A further example of institutional bias is offered by public choice theory, for that is explicitly about openly competitive systems of government and about influences on voting behaviour.

Although far from being an homogeneous class of economies, many ldcs remain sufficiently 'different' from dcs for care to be needed when exporting the policy recommendations of mainstream theory from the latter to the former. 'Dualism' summarises a good deal of the difference. This refers to various asymmetries of production and organisation which, *inter alia*, prevent productivities from being equalised at the margin and

---

73. Helleiner, 1988 pp.25-26, draws attention to the overt value bias in interest rate theory in its implicit denial of Islamic teachings on this subject and points out that accumulating environmental concerns are making zero, or at least very low, discount rates look less irrational than economics would have us believe.

resources from moving freely. Thus, McKinnon [1973 p.5] has written of 'severe fragmentation in the underdeveloped economy' in the sense that enterprises and households are so isolated that they face different effective prices for commodities and factors. One illustration of this is the large differences which commonly exist between interest rates in the formal and informal credit markets, implying both different sources of loanable funds in the two sub-markets and that different groups use these sub-markets to meet their credit needs.[74] Labour markets in ldcs are also often marked by dualism, with non-equalising relationships between the formal and informal, or traditional, segments. While there is no longer any doubt that people in ldcs respond 'normally' to pecuniary incentives, this is not to say that traditional or institutional factors — such as extended family arrangements or divisions of labour based on gender, race or caste — do not sometimes dampen or modify that response.[75]

In other respects too markets in ldcs are generally characterised by greater 'imperfections' than in dcs, although this is admittedly to generalise on too grand a scale. It is still common for widely differing prices to exist for the same product in outlets geographically close to each other, implying failures of information and/or competition. Although there is a paucity of research on this, it seems likely that there is considerably greater industrial concentration in ldcs when compared with dcs, with an associated probability of larger monopoly powers.[76] Substantial imperfections still exist in many labour markets, making it difficult to handle them well within a neoclassical framework,[77] and while much emphasis has been placed in recent years on 'financially repressive' policies of governments in many ldcs, the IMF is among those who point out that much state 'interference' in capital markets has

---

74. See Addison and Demery, 1987, for a brief review of the literature on dualism in financial markets.

75. See Lele, 1988, on this subject as applied to rural labour responses in Africa, who points out [p.197] that, 'The neoclassical assumption of maximisation of a joint household utility function determining household labour allocation is contradicted by such gender-based divisions of labour, especially where polygamous situations prevail.'

76. See Killick, 1981, chapt. 10 for a statement of this argument. Casson and Pearce, 1987, provide a recent study of the effect of multinational corporations on industrial concentration but they also note the shortage of hard evidence on concentration in ldcs.

77. See Berry's 1987 survey of the literature on labour markets in ldcs, especially p.217.

partly been prompted by monopolistic or oligopolistic behaviour by banks, or by other major imperfections in those markets.[78] It can finally be added that high transactions costs resulting from the underdeveloped institutional framework of the economy mean that markets are less complete in most ldcs. This is likely to be particularly true of markets for various financial instruments, for transport and marketing services, for information and for forward markets of all kinds, and is liable to have particularly adverse effects on the efficiency and expansion of traditional forms of production.[79]

*   *   *

From considerations such as those presented in this chapter some writers have drawn very negative conclusions about the usefulness of mainstream theory for the design of economic policies in ldcs. Rashid, for example, argues that 'developments in economic theory have not proved helpful in guiding economic policy. Nor can this situation be expected to improve.'[80] Such is *not* the position taken here. I should similarly like to distance myself from the reactions of the non-economists in a multi-disciplinary seminar discussion of an earlier version of this monograph who joyfully interpreted it as an attack on the relevance of economics! Quite to the contrary, the following section points out a number of ways in which contemporary mainstream thinking has direct relevance to ldc policy problems

The purpose of this chapter has rather been to draw attention to the often fragile bases of policy recommendations which nevertheless are commonly presented in highly confident, not to say dogmatic, fashion; and to argue the case for more caution and modesty in making such prescriptions. Implicitly, it is an argument for the continuing need for a 'development economics', which can

---

78. IMF, 1983, p.3. It is also interesting that one of its prime advocates has recently qualified his espousal of the liberalisation of capital markets in the light of recent experience. See McKinnon, 1988, pp.407-9. See also Fry, 1982, especially p.746, on the dangers of applying equilibrium models to analyses of ldc financial markets.
79. See Myint, 1985, on incomplete markets arising from institutional deficiencies, and Arndt's 1988 discussion of this. Lele, 1988, pp.196-204 provides various examples of incomplete markets in the rural economies of Africa.
80. Rashid, 1988 p.207. He is particularly concerned with the limitations imposed by theorists' preoccupation with mathematical methods and the resulting neglect of historical, institutional and other qualitative considerations, and of 'intuition'.

undertake the tasks of adapting mainstream normative economics to developing country circumstances and can focus far more than the mainstream does on dynamic processes of change and development.

5
Using Contemporary Theory

If the profession were able to summon up such uncharacteristic qualities as caution and modesty, what then might be learned from mainstream theoretical developments for the design of policies in developing countries?

Applications of contemporary normative economics

The Superiority of the Long View: First, there are many resonances between the policy needs of ldcs and the stress in contemporary macroeconomics, noted earlier, on the importance of taking a long-term view, and of the management of supply as well as demand. Indeed, development economists have in the past complained about the preoccupation of the International Monetary Fund with demand management in its stand-by programmes and have urged greater attention to structural weaknesses; in turn, the Fund has introduced more supply-side measures into its programmes in the 1980s.[81] It and, more particularly, the World Bank also now support many programmes of 'structural adjustment' which attempt to look beyond immediate crisis-management and pay attention to strengthening the productive system.[82]

The Macro-micro Distinction: The conclusion of macroeconomists in industrial countries that the results of a given set of policies in the longer term may be both different from, and worse than, their short term effects is also highly pertinent. This applies directly to the pursuit of expansionary 'full employment' macro policies and their longer-term effects on inflation and expectations, and more

---

81. See Killick et al, 1984, especially chapts. 6 and 8, for a critique along these lines and an espousal of a "real economy" approach.
82. See Corbo et al, 1987, for a discussion of these and related issues.

generally to ad hoc decisions, say on protecting local industries, which may appear to make good short-term sense but which in aggregate might eventually have severely adverse results.

Expectations: One of the consequences of the RE and NCM counter-revolutions in macroeconomics has been to erode the distinction between 'macro' and 'micro' theory and, in particular, to insist that macroeconomics should have firm micro foundations.[83] This too should be welcomed in the context of ldcs, where the 'big' macro problem is to expand productive capabilities, and is closely related to the observation above about the need for adequate supply-side policies in adjustment programmes.[84] There is relevance too in the modern emphasis on the importance for macro policy of the ways in which factor markets work, the speed with which they clear, and interventions to improve their efficiency — particularly in economies characterised by dualism in capital and labour markets. The unavailability of the interest rate as an equilibrating variable in financially 'repressed' systems may, for example, impose substantial costs.

On the face of it, the RE approach has limited direct applicability, for its extremely demanding assumptions about access to information (and implicitly about the level of educational sophistication of the populace) seem particularly inappropriate for conditions in many ldcs. The standard conclusion that demand management measures can only work if they can surprise private agents because they are unsystematic, or if they can be more flexible — changed more often — than wages are not central to macro-policy problems in many ldcs. As Corden [1987, p.177] has suggested, greater political instability in ldcs, and lower levels of coherence and predictability in macro policies, mean that the special concern of the RE school with the anticipation of systematic policies is less relevant.

---

83. Long ago Arrow [1967] called it a "major scandal" that neoclassical price theory could not account for such macro phenomena as persistent, large-scale unemployment; and Lucas and Sargent [1979] argued that Keynesian macroeconomics was 'fundamentally flawed' by its lack of firm micro foundations.
84. In addition to the familiar macro-micro distinction, we should note too the idea of a 'meso' dimension presented by Cornia et al, 1987, chapt. 6. Writing in the context of the design of structural adjustment, they see meso policies as measures mediating the effects of macro policies on income distribution and the living standards of the poor.

The debate about expectations is, however, highly pertinent to ldcs in drawing attention to the importance of the way people react to — and seek to anticipate — government actions, and to the techniques the public develops for accommodating or frustrating those policies. The general consensus in the literature on the importance of incorporating expectations into the design of macro policy and that this importance increases as policy objectives become longer-term is particularly to the point. The ways in which public reactions can undermine policy intentions will admittedly often differ between dcs and ldcs. In the former, particular attention has focussed on the behaviour of the [formal sector, wage] labour market and the emergence of the vertical Phillips curve; in developing countries it is more through the growth of parallel markets and corruption that the people's reactions can frustrate the policy-makers. But the analogy is valid. More generally, the insistence of modern macro theory on the necessity in designing policies of taking into account how people are likely to react to them is salutary in drawing attention to the importance, therefore, of the *credibility* of government measures. Many measures come unstuck because people simply do not believe the government is willing or able to make them stick.

Crowding-out: Another relevant concept arising from the anti-Keynesian counter-revolution is that of 'crowding out'. In mainstream macro theory this chiefly refers to ways in which private saving and expenditure behaviour frustrates government attempts to manipulate aggregate demand [see p.11], which is less relevant to conditions in many ldcs, but the related notion of *financial* crowding out is certainly pertinent. This can be said to occur when increased public sector borrowing results in reduced credit to the private sector, because higher interest rates are induced or through some other credit rationing mechanism.[85] There are many ldcs which have had such experiences.

The Dutch Disease: The literature on the Dutch Disease is another aspect of recent theory with relevance to a significant number of ldcs.[86] This shows how a sector which is large and expanding

85. See Feltenstein, 1986, on financial crowding out. He draws attention to the possibility of some secondary crowding-out effects as a result of reduced private sector activity, in addition to the primary effect described above.
86. See Cordon, 1984b, for an up-to-date survey of this literature. See also van Wijnbergen, 1984. Roemer, 1985, provides an insightful discussion of the uses and limitations of this literature in ldc circumstances.

rapidly relative to the rest of the economy, typically as the result of a natural resource discovery, can attract resources from, and impose contraction on, traditional producers of tradeable goods by causing a real appreciation of the exchange rate and through other mechanisms. It is true that the theory has a relatively short-term focus and would need modification when applied to long-run development, and that the ways in which the processes work themselves out would be somewhat different in many ldc circumstances. But much of the thrust of the theory — and its policy recommendation that subsidisation of the lagging sectors is justified in certain circumstances — remains highly pertinent to major ldc producers of oil and other mineral products.

The Assignment Rule: Also highly pertinent, and in this case of general applicability, is the development in the theory of economic policy known as the 'assignment rule'.[87] This states that the net benefits of a policy measure will usually be greater when it is targeted directly at the distortion which is the cause of the policy intervention. The more indirectly the policy works the more likely it is that it will itself create additional distortions. This principle has mainly been used in discussions of trade policy, to argue that protectionism is almost never an optimal policy response because most economic arguments for protection refer to causes *domestic* in nature and are thus better redressed by subsidies, taxation or other domestic measures. On this view, protection is only generally a preferred intervention in the face of causes relating specifically to the conditions of international trade, as in the case of optimal tariff theory. However, the assignment rule is in principle a general one, with potentially important applications to a wide range of economic policies in dcs and ldcs alike. Unfortunately, there appear so far to have been few applications outside the trade policy context.

DUPs: Perhaps better known and of particular relevance of ldc conditions is the theory of directly unproductive profitseeking (DUP) activities and rent seeking, reported earlier [see p.13]. Besides drawing attention to such activities as an additional cost of government interventions, the main policy thrust of this theory has been to recommend the abolition or reduction of price and

---

87. See especially Corden, 1974; also Bliss, 1987.

quantitative controls and other non-market interventions which create opportunities and incentives for DUPs, including corruption. However, as suggested earlier [p.26], it also constitutes an additional case *for* policy interventions when market imperfections lead to the existence or possibility of monopoly rents in the private sector. Either way, the theory of DUPs has made a valuable contribution to the design of economic policy.

The theory of trade policy

We should also consider the current state of theory bearing upon trade policy, which has so far been little discussed in this monograph. Recent decades have seen a variety of new trends in international commerce and the need to take cognisance of these in the literature has resulted in a large volume of work known loosely as New Trade Theory. Among the developments to which these writers have been responding have been (a) the relative growth in trade between similar economies, e.g. through the European Community; (b) the increased extent of two-way trade, with industrial countries both importing and exporting similar goods such, as cars; (c) the relative growth of intra-firm trade across national borders by transnational corporations; (d) the growth of counter-trade; (e) the increased importance of scale economies in production, and other forces making for less than perfect competition.[88]

Particular attention has been paid to the implications for trade policy of returns to scale and imperfect competition.[89] Although there is a venerable literature on scale economies, the existence of such has been developed into a 'new' argument for protection. In the absence of outside competition the home producer can move down his cost curve by increasing output and this may get him to the point where he becomes internationally competitive and no longer needs protection. On the other hand, since scale economies create natural monopolies, the case for free trade might be said to be strengthened as a safeguard of consumer interests against the exploitation of monopoly power and as widening the range of choice available to them. In either case, it is clear that trade and anti-monopoly policies should be designed together.

---

88. See Bliss, 1987, for some discussion of this and of the policy implications of the new trade theory. Also Kierzkowski, 1984 and 1987, and Krugman, 1987.
89. See Venables and Smith, 1987, for an exploration of this subject.

External economies resulting from investments in knowledge provide another 'new' argument for protection, arising from incomplete appropriability of the benefits of R & D, the argument being that protection could compensate for this non-appropriability and thus avoid sub-optimal levels of private investment in knowledge. A somewhat similar set of consideration arises from the learning benefits that might be derived from a protection-induced import substitution, for example in the development of an indigenous technological capacity [Bruton, 1987]. There has similarly been recent theoretical interest in the circumstances in which export subsidies might be justified, although the budgetary demands that these would make on the revenues and the dangers of provoking retaliation limit the practicability of this instrument.[90]

Another familiar conclusion common to old and new trade theory is that the desirability or otherwise of free trade depends on whether the objective function is to maximise the welfare of the world or of the nation. This has long been understood in the case of the 'optimum' tariff, through which a large trading country increases national welfare by exploiting its monopoly power through trade restrictions, but at the cost of a greater welfare loss by the rest of the world. This also applies with restrictions to allow home producers to enjoy greater use of economies of scale: the home economy may benefit (so long as there is no retaliation) but only at the expense of its trading partners.

While this remains a highly contentious area, the prevailing view appears to be that, while the new trade theory has yielded additional theoretical grounds upon which rational arguments for protectionism, export subsidies and other measures which depart from the free trade principle can be based, it does not provide an adequate basis for advocating trade restrictions. In this sense, the broadly free (or freer) trade stance of the economics profession remains. There is also greater confidence that the Hekscher-Ohlin model of comparative advantage can provide an at least approximate explanation of actual trading patterns, which also reinforces the traditional stance of the profession.[91] It is a more

---

90. See, for example, Brander and Spencer, 1985. Also Sachs, 1987, and the comment by Bhagwati, same volume, pp.283-84.
91. The so-called 'Leontief paradox' [1953] was based on evidence which appeared to show that the USA imported capital-intensive and exported labour-intensive goods, in apparent contradiction of the Hekscher-Ohlin factor-proportions version of comparative advantage theory. This result stimulated much effort to undertake further tests. It is not possible to review this literature here and there are many

complicated stance, however. It draws upon the studies of the political-economy of protectionism to point out that it is easy for the analytically correct arguments of the economist to be perverted by commercial interests into 'bad' policies; it uses the assignment rule to argue that protection is rarely the optimal policy intervention for dealing with a domestic distortion; and it adopts a more worldly caution about the policy advice it offers. Krugman [1987, p.143] catches the mood exactly:

> The economic cautions about the difficulty of formulating useful interventions and the political economy concerns that interventionism may go astray combine into a new case for free trade. This is not the old case that free trade is optimal because markets are efficient. Instead, it is a sadder but wiser argument for free trade as a rule of thumb in a world whose politics are as imperfect as its markets.
>
> The economic cautions are crucial to this argument. If the potential gains from interventionist trade policies were large, it would be hard to argue against making some effort to realise these gains. [But]...the gains from intervention are limited by uncertainty about appropriate policies, by entry that dissipates the gains, and by the general equilibrium effects that insure that promoting one sector diverts resources from others. The combination of these factors limits the potential benefits of sophisticated interventions.
>
> Once the expected gains from intervention have been whittled down sufficiently, political economy can be invoked as a reason to forego intervention altogether. Free trade can serve as a focal point on which countries can agree to avoid trade wars. It can also serve as a simple principle with which to resist pressures of special-interest politics. To abandon the free trade principle in pursuit of the gains from sophisticated intervention could therefore open the door to adverse political consequences that would outweigh the potential gains.
>
> It is possible, then, both to believe that comparative advantage is an incomplete model of trade and to believe that free trade is nevertheless the right policy. In fact, this is the position taken by most new trade theorists themselves. So free trade is not passé' — but it is not what it once was.

methodological pitfalls in the way of adequate testing, but the balance of the evidence seems broadly supportive of the view that, after distinctions are made between different levels of skill and other differentiations, much of the pattern of trade is explained by differences in factor proportions. Leamer's, 1984, study is probably the most thorough and sophisticated; it concludes [p.xvi] that his tests show that 'Hekscher-Ohlin comes out looking rather well.' A good deal of trade is apparently explained by differences in physical and human capital, labour and natural resources, although his tests were unable to capture the influence of enterprise and other 'animal spirits'.

While we have already remarked on the unsatisfactorily static nature of trade theory and there certainly are forces in the working-out of comparative advantage which operate to the disadvantage of developing countries,[92] such policy caution is certainly pertinent to ldcs, where, indeed, governments' ability to withstand the sophistries of special interest groups may often be less than in dcs. Moreover, it could be argued that, being more realistic, new trade theory is more relevant as a basis for policy advice to these countries than the 'pure' comparative advantage model.

---

92. See Stewart, 1984, for a thoughtful discussion of these in the light of new trade theory, but she too is cautious about advocating protectionism by ldcs.

6
Conclusion

Implications for aid donors

One of the motives for writing this monograph was concern about the much increased influence within developing countries of mainstream thinking about economic policy, effected chiefly through the vehicle of the policy 'conditionality' of the Bretton Woods lenders and, to a lesser extent, bilateral aid donors — and the danger that it is unwittingly being applied in inappropriate ways. The economic difficulties of the indebted countries of Africa and Latin America has left them highly susceptible to the policy 'advice' of the donor community, leading to an historically unprecedented explosion of conditionality in these regions in recent years. What are the implications of the foregoing for the design of conditionality?

Perhaps implicit in the discussion has been the premise that economic policy matters — that for good or ill it can have a decisive influence on countries' abilities to satisfy the material aspirations of their citizens.[93] If this be accepted, it follows that the effectiveness of aid — if the motive is to raise the pace of development, as distinct from the other motives associated with aid — will be crucially affected by the quality of the policy environment into which it is introduced.[94] In turn, it follows from this that donor governments have a legitimate interest in the economic policies of recipient governments; it is this, the scarcity of aid resources and their opportunity costs which justify policy 'conditionality' — always assuming that it can actually achieve what it seeks to do. Precisely one of the chief influences that led the World Bank to become increasingly involved in 'policy-related' lending was that it was finding that many of the development projects in which it had invested in the past were failing, not because of any inherent design flaws but because the policy environment in which they were operating prevented them from generating the returns, the contributions to development, which had been expected. What, in this case, are the implications of our arguments for the content of conditionality, for example in the design of adjustment programmes? Some 'dos' and 'don'ts' suggest themselves.

First, the way in which the public sector goes about its tasks is more important than its absolute size. We have argued that the role of the state should be the incidental outcome of the relative efficiencies of each sector and will vary greatly from country to country. We envisage, however, that in most ldcs application of this principle would leave a major role for the state. Arndt [1988 pp.227-28] provides one reason for this:

> Markets, it has been said, work incrementally. All required changes — in price signals, in people's response to incentives, in shifts of resources — take time. These lags account for the fact that elasticities of supply and demand are larger in the long than in the short run. Even in Western market economies, it has been recognised that very large changes that have to be accomplished quickly, such as the conversion of a peace to a war economy, cannot be left to a market economy. The likelihood of market failure therefore is a function of the degree of urgency — or impatience — attached to a particular change. The *prime facie* case for government action to promote development in underdeveloped countries rests largely on the belief that what is needed is *rapid* economic development, the

---

93. Krueger, 1987, examines the degree of influence of policy in a comparison of the post-war economic histories of South Korea and Turkey and concludes [p.173] that 'Out of this contrast, the lesson that "policies matter" emerges clearly.' Even though Turkey apparently started with natural advantages, she argues that superior economic policies have left Korea in a far better economic situation today, with contrasting trade policies having been particularly crucial. The comparison is similarly sometimes made between the post-Independence records of Ghana and Cote d'Ivoire, with the superior economic performance of the latter usually explained in terms of the different policy stances of the two countries over most the post-Independence years. See also Reynolds, 1983 p.976, who argues that the single most important indicator of variations in growth among ldcs is 'political organisation and the administrative competence of government.' At a different level, we may judge the importance of policy by comparing alternative scenarios from forecasting models with and without policy changes. This type of exercise is regularly undertaken, for example, in the World Bank's annual *World Development Report*. Thus its 1987 edition [pp.24-27] provides 'high' and 'low' scenarios differentiated by countries' policy responses to their adjustment problems. It finds large differences in world and regional growth rates, and in trade and balance of payments outcomes depending on these responses.
94. See Riddell, 1987 chapt. 10, for material relating to this and the references cited there.

compression into a few decades of a process that in the West took centuries.

This consideration has all the greater force in the dire circumstances in which most structural adjustment programmes are formulated. What matters more than its absolute size is how the state goes about its tasks and what relationships it establishes with the private sector — to the extent that a clear distinction can be drawn between them. The key task is to establish working relationships between the sectors which, so far as possible, are mutually supportive rather than antagonistic.

Second, to the extent that policy interventions are necessary, it is better that they should work with, or through, market forces than against them. Indeed, it is more than likely that failure will attend policies which seek to swim against the tide of market incentives. At the same time, however, recognise the limitations of narrowly market-oriented programmes; and the potentially wide range of 'market failures' which would justify government intervention, if there is reasonable cause to believe that this will result in a net improvement in welfare. Relatedly, we have stressed the symbiotic nature of relationships between the public and private sectors, and the key importance of establishing mutually supportive policies.

Third, beware the temptation of exaggerating the appropriateness of policy prescriptions derived from mainstream theory, and the over-confident advocacy of those prescriptions which such exaggeration can cause. We have urged caution and modesty because of the value biases of the mainstream; the frequent lack of consensus within the profession; the particular limitations associated with the dominant neo-classical school; and the contextual bias of mainstream theory towards conditions in the advanced economies of the West. In particular, avoid simplistic and single-solution responses to complex problems and economic systems. Serious economic problems are usually complicated and so too are the ways in which specific interventions work their ways through an economy.[95] In similar vein, beware the temptation to apply similar prescriptions across countries. It has become a commonplace to observe the great diversity among the countries we choose to call 'developing'; their specific characteristics and circumstances vary greatly, as also the effects on their economies of a given type of policy intervention.[96] Within the limitations imposed by these cautions, however, policies should obviously make the fullest possible use of modern economic knowledge. Chapter 5 gives a partial list of specific applications and it is noteworthy that many of them are nowadays incorporated in adjustment programmes: an emphasis on the supply side of the economy; on measures that will improve the workings of key markets; of avoiding and reducing rent-seeking activities and other distortions created by government interventions; taking greater advantage of international trade and reducing levels of protection. In many country situations, measures along these lines are likely to bring improvements, always provided that they are part of a more broadly-based and pragmatic response tailored to specific country situations.

A last 'don't': do not forget the politics of policy reform. By the act of laying down policy conditions aid donors willy-nilly become active players in the domestic politics of the recipient country. As such, however, their power to bring about major change is usually very circumscribed and they operate at many disadvantages. The key question is whether there is a constituency, or coalition, for reform within the country to which the donors can then lend their support. The danger is that donors will use their muscle in ways which have political consequences which they are not in a position to anticipate and whose risks will have to be borne by others. Many apparently irrational economic policy interventions have a strong political logic, so that reversal of these could create destabilising political vacuums.[97] When faced with such dangers, government will resist the policy leverage of donor agencies; and the evidence suggests that when they do so conditionality is unlikely to effect much real change.

---

95. Some of the flavour of the complexity is provided by the following extract from Lele, 1988 p.204, writing about policies towards Africa's rural economy: 'To summarise, the incentives for export crop production involve a complex set of issues typically overlooked in general economic discussions, which have tended to focus almost exclusively on the producer price levels.....reliance on markets may not necessarily ensure competitive processing or marketing of crops, where monopolies exist, or where historical factors explain oligopolistic tendencies. African reluctance to relinquish public control of such activities is perhaps explained more by concerns of ethnic rivalries and consequent political instability than by ideological considerations. This suggests that donor emphasis on precipitating market liberalisation in the short run may well set back the cause of market development.'
96. The literature on comparative economic systems stresses the diversity which is found and the uniqueness, therefore, of individual economies — see Gottlieb, 1984.

One of the implications of the above do's and don'ts is that conditionality is a tricky and labour-intensive business. Regional development banks, the aid arm of the European Community and bilateral donors who may wish to get into it have to be willing and able to devote considerable manpower and other resources to it. Few, if any, of them have such resources. For this reason as well as to avoid foreign policy complications, the common practice of 'piggy-backing' on the conditionality of the Bretton Woods institutions makes good sense. However, this could leave the Bretton Woods agencies with a dangerous monopoly of expertise and a great deal hinges on whether their conditionality is well designed, flexible, sensitive, etc. There remains much controversy on this and the evidence for the effectiveness of their programmes is less than compelling.

If indeed they decide to piggy-back, then bilateral and other agencies must satisfy themselves about the appropriateness of the Bretton Woods policy designs. This task itself demands resources and expertise. To the extent that they are dissatisfied with the policies, the piggy-backers must seek to influence the multilateral institutions to remedy felt deficiencies. This, in turn, requires that there be effective mechanisms in place through which such influence can be exerted, although there would inevitably be resistance to such encroachments. In any case, it is perhaps in assessing the policies of the Bretton Woods institutions that the rules suggested in this section might most appropriately be applied.

---

97. Thus Sandbrook, 1986 p.330, writing about Africa argues that although policies to reduce the role of the state and increase the influence of market forces are "plausible" they are also "ahistorical and apolitical". It is apolitical because "the suggested changes would undercut the power and/or wealth of political insiders." What, he asks, will hold societies together when rulers have little patronage to dispense in countries where the 'pre-eminent problem [is] how to rule unintegrated peasant societies.' See also footnote 95.

Bibliography

Addison, T. and Demery, L. 1987, *Monetary Control in Developing Countries*. London: Overseas Development Institute, November (mimeo).

Allison, G.T. 1971, *Essence of Decision: Explaining the Cuban Missile Crisis*. Boston: Little Brown & Co.

Alt, J.E. and Chrystal, K.A. 1983, *Political Economics*. Brighton: Wheatsheaf Books.

Arndt, H.W. 1988, '"Market failure" and underdevelopment', *World Development*, 16(2); February.

Arrow, K.J. 1951, *Social Choice and Individual Values*. New York: Wiley.

Arrow, K.J. 1967, 'Samuelson collected', *Journal of Political Economy*, 75; October.

Arrow, K.J. 1971, *Essays in the Theory of Risk Bearing*. Amsterdam: North-Holland.

Arrow, K.J. 1987, 'Arrow's theorem', in Eatwell et al (eds).

Baldwin, R.E. 1984, 'Trade policies in developed countries', in Jones and Kenen (eds), Vol.I, chapter 12.

Barro, R. 1974, 'Are government bonds net wealth?', *Journal of Political Economy*, 82(6).

Bates, R.H. 1981, *Markets and States in Tropical Africa*. Berkeley: University of California Press.

Bauer, R.A. 1968, 'The study of policy formation: an introduction', in R.A. Bauer and K.J. Gergen (eds), *The Study of Policy Formation*. New York: Free Press.

Baumol, W.J.; Panzar, J.C.; and Willig, R.D. 1982, *Contestable Markets and the Theory of Industry Structure*. New York: Harcourt Brace Jovanovich.

Baumol, W.J.; Panzar, J.C.; and Willig, R.D. 1985, 'On the theory of perfectly contestable markets', in J. Stiglitz and F. Mathewson (eds), *New Developments in the Analysis of Market Structure*. New York: Harcourt Brace.

Baumol, W.J. and Willig, R.D. (forthcoming), 'New developments in contestability theory', *Oxford Economic Papers*.

Begg, D.; Fischer, S.; and Dornbusch, R. 1987, *Economics* (2nd edition). London: McGraw Hill.

Berlin, I. 1969, 'Two concepts of liberty', in his *Four Essays on Liberty*, Oxford University Press.

Berry, A. 1987, 'The labour market and human capital in ldcs', in Gemmell (ed), chapter 6.

Bhagwati, J.N. 1982, 'Directly unproductive profit-seeking (DUP) activities', *Journal of Political Economy*, 90; October.

Bhagwati, J.N. and Srinivasan, T.N. 1983, *Lectures on International Trade*. Cambridge, Massachusetts: MIT Press.

Bliss, C. 1987, 'The new trade theory and economic policy', *Oxford Review of Economic Policy*, 3(1); Spring.

Bhom, P. 1987, 'Second best', in Eatwell et al (eds), Vol.4, pp.280-84.

Booth, D. 1987, 'Alternatives in the restructuring of state-society relations: research issues for tropical Africa', *IDS Bulletin*, 18(4); October.

Brander, J.A. and Spencer, B.J. 1985, 'Export subsidies and international market share rivalry', *Journal of International Economics*, 18.

Bruton, H. 1987, 'Technology choice and factor proportions problems in ldcs', in Gemmell (ed), op.cit.

Buchanan, J. and Tullock, G. 1962, *The Calculus of Consent: Logical Foundations of Constitutional Democracy*, Ann Arbor: University of Michigan Press.

Buiter, W.H. 1985, 'A guide to public sector debts and deficits', *Economic Policy*, 1(1); November.

Caldwell, B.J. (ed) 1984, *Appraisal and Criticism in Economics*. London: Allen and Unwin.

Casson, M. and Pearce, R.D. 1987, 'Multinational enterprises in LDCs', in Gemmell (ed).

Chenery, H.B. 1975, 'The structuralist approach to development policy', *American Economic Review Papers and Proceedings*, LXV(2); May.

Chenery, H.B. 1988, 'Structural transformation: a program of research', in G. Ranis and T.P. Schultz (eds), chapter 3.

Chenery, H.; Ahluwalia, M.S.; Bell, C.L.G.; Duloy, J.H.; and Jolly, R. (eds) 1974, *Redistribution With Growth*. London: Oxford University Press.

Clark, J.M. 1940, 'Towards a concept of workable competition', *American Economic Review*; June.

Colander, D.C. and Klamer, A. 1987, 'The making of an economist', *Journal of Economic Perspectives*, 1(2); Fall.

Cook, P. and Kirkpatrick, C. (eds) 1988, *Privatisation in Less Developed Countries*. Brighton: Wheatsheaf Books.

Corbo, V.; Goldstein, M.; and Khan, M. (eds) 1987, *Growth-Oriented Adjustment Programs*. Washington: IMF and World Bank.

Corden, W.M. 1974, *Trade Policy and Economic Welfare*, Oxford University Press.

Corden, W. M. 1984a, 'The normative theory of international trade', in Jones and Kenen (eds), Vol.I, chapter 2.

Corden, W. M. 1984b, 'Booming sector and Dutch Disease economics: survey and consolidation', *Oxford Economic Papers*, 36(3); November.

Corden, W. M. 1987, 'The relevance for developing countries of recent developments in macroeconomic theory', *World Bank Research Observer*, 2(2); July.

Cornia, G.A.; Jolly, R.; Stewart, F. (eds) 1987, *Adjustment with a Human Face: Protecting the Vulnerable and Promoting Growth*. Oxford University Press.

Dasgupta, P. 1986, 'Positive freedom, markets and the welfare state', *Oxford Review of Economic Policy*, 2(2); Summer.

Deane, P. 1983, 'The scope and method of economic science', *Economic Journal*, 93(369); March.

Dearlove, J. 1987, 'Economists on the state', *IDS Bulletin*, 18(3); July.

Dearlove, J. and White, G. 1987, 'The retreat of the state? Editorial introduction', *IDS Bulletin*, 18(3); July.

Downs, A. 1957, *An Economic Analysis of Democracy*. New York: Harper and Row.

Dutkiewicz, P. and Williams, G. 1987, 'All the King's horses and all the King's men couldn't put Humpty-Dumpty together again', *IDS Bulletin*, 18(3); July.

Eatwell, J.; Milgate, M.; and Newman, P. (eds) 1987, *The New Palgrove Dictionary of Economics* (4 vols). London: Macmillan Press.

Feltenstein, A. 1986, 'Financial crowding-out: theory with an application to Australia', *IMF Staff Papers*, 33(1); March.

Findlay, R. 1988, 'Trade, development and the state', in Ranis and Schultz (eds), chapter 4.

Fischer, S. 1987, 'New classical macroeconomics', in Eatwell et al, Vol.3, pp.647-51.

Fischer, S. 1988, 'Recent developments in macroeconomics', *Economic Journal*, 98(391); June.

Fisher, F.M. 1983, *Disequilibrium Foundations of Equilibrium Economics*, Cambridge University Press.

Friedman, B.M. 1979, 'Optimal expectations and the extreme information assumptions of "rational" expectations models', *Journal of Monetary Economics* 5.

Friedman, M. 1968, 'The role of monetary policy', *American Economic Review*, 58; March.

Friedman, M. 1970, *The Counter-Revolution in Monetary Theory*. London: Institute of Economic Affairs.

Fry, M.J. 1982, 'Models of financially repressed developing economies', *World Development*, 10(9); September.

Gemmell, N. (ed) 1987, *Surveys in Development Economics*. Oxford: Basil Blackwell.

Gottlieb, M. 1984, *Theory of Economic Systems*. Orlando: Academic Press.

Greenaway, D. and Milner, C. 1987, 'Trade theory and the less developed countries', in Gemmell (ed), chapter 1.

Griffin, K. and Gurley, J. 1985, 'Radical analyses of imperialism, the Third World and the transition to socialism: a survey article', *Journal of Economic Literature*, XXIII(3); September.

Hahn, F.H. 1987, 'Neoclassical growth theory', in Eatwell et al, Vol.3, pp.625-34.

Haltiwanger, J. 1987, 'Natural rate of unemployment', in Eatwell, et al, Vol.3, pp.610-12.

Hanke, S.H. (ed) 1987, *Prospects for Privatization*. New York: Academy for Political Science.

Hanke, S.H. (ed) 1987, *Privatization and Development*. San Francisco: ICS Press.

Heal, G.M. 1973, *The Theory of Economic Planning*. Amsterdam: North-Holland.

Helleiner, G.K. 1981, 'The Refsnes seminar: economic theory and North-South negotiations', *World Development*, 9(6); June.

Helleiner, G.K. 1988, 'Conventional foolishness and overall ignorance: current approaches to global transformation and development', University of Toronto (mimeo); June.

Helm, D. 1986, 'The assessment: the economic borders of the state', *Oxford Review of Economic Policy*, 2(2); Summer.

Hicks, Sir John 1965, *Capital and Growth*. Oxford: Oxford University Press.

Hicks, J. 1979, *Causality in Economics*. New York: Basic Books.

Hirschman, A.O. 1982, 'The rise and decline of development economics', in Gersovitz, Diaz-Alejandro, Ranis and Rosenzweig (eds), *The Theory and Experience of Economic Development*. London: Allen and Unwin.

Inman, R.P. 1985, 'Markets, governments and the 'new' political economy', in Alan J. Auerbach and Martin Feldstein (eds), *Handbook of Public Economics*, Vol.II, chapter 12. Amsterdam: North-Holland.

International Monetary Fund 1983, *Interest Rate Policies in Developing Countries*. Washington: IMF Occasional Paper No.22; October.

Jackson, R.H. and Rosberg, C.G. 1984, 'Personal rule: theory and practice in Africa', *Comparative Politics*, 16(4); July.

Jones, R.W. and Kenen, P.B. (eds) 1984, *Handbook of International Economics* (2 vols). Amsterdam: North-Holland.

Judd, J.P. and Scadding, J.L. 1982, 'The search for a stable money demand function: a survey of the post-1973 literature', *Journal of Economic Literature*, 20; September.

Hendry, D.F. and Ericsson, N.R. 1983, 'Assertion without empirical basis: an econometric appraisal of Friedman and Schwartz, 'Monetary trends in ... the United Kingdom'. London: Bank of England; October.

Kaldor, N. 1972, 'The irrelevance of equilibrium economics', *Economic Journal*, 82(328); December.

Kamien, M.I. 1987, 'Market structure and innovation', in Eatwell et al, Vol.3, pp.345-47.

Kamien, M.I. and Schwarz, N.L. 1982, *Market Structure and Innovation*, Cambridge University Press.

Kay, J.A. and Thompson, D.J. 1986, 'Privatisation: a policy in search of a rationale', *Economic Journal*, 96; March.

Kendrick, D.A. 1988, *Feedback: A New Framework for Macroeconomic Policy*. Amsterdam: Kluwer Academic Publishers.

Kierzkowski, H. (ed) 1984, *Monopolistic Competition and International Trade*, Oxford University Press.

Kierzkowski, H. (ed) 1987, *Protection and Competition in International Trade*. Oxford: Basil Blackwell.

Kierzkowski, H. 1987, 'Recent advances in international trade theory: a selective survey', *Oxford Review of Economic Policy*, 3(1); Spring.

Killick, T. 1976, 'The possibilities of development planning', *Oxford Economic Papers*; July.

Killick, T. 1981, *Policy Economics*. London: Heinemann Educational Books.

Killick, T. (ed) 1984, *The Quest for Economic Stabilisation: the IMF and the Third World*. London: Overseas Development Institute and Gower Publishing Co.

Killick, T. 1986, 'Twenty-five years in development: the rise and impending decline of market solutions', *Development Policy Review*, 4(2); June.

Killick, T. 1988, 'Wither development economics?' Presidential address to the Development Studies Association. London: Overseas Development Institute; September (mimeo).

Krueger, A.O. 1974, 'The political economy of the rent-seeking society', *American Economic Review*, 64; June.

Krueger, A.O. 1984, 'Trade policies in developing countries', in Jones and Kenen, op.cit., Vol.I, chapter II.

Krueger, A.O. 1987, 'The importance of economic policy in development: contrasts between Korea and Turkey', in Kierzkowski (ed).

Krugman, P.R. 1987, 'Is Free Trade passe?', *Journal of Economic Perspectives*, 1(2); Fall.

Lafont, J.J. 1987, 'Externalities', in Eatwell et al (eds); Vol.2, pp.263-65.

Lal, D. 1983, *The Poverty of 'Development Economics'*. London: Institute of Economic Affairs.

Lal, D. 1984, 'The political economy of the predatory state'. London: University College Discussion Paper 84-12. See also his *The Hindu Equilibrium*, Oxford University Press (forthcoming).

Lamb, G. 1987, *Managing Economic Policy Change: Institutional Dimensions*, World Bank Discussion Paper No.14, Washington; June.

Leamer, E.E. 1984, *Sources of International Comparative Advantage: Theory and Evidence*. Cambridge, Massachusetts: MIT Press.

Leibenstein, H. 1966, 'Allocative efficiency vs. "X-efficiency"', *American Economic Review*, 56; June.

Leibenstein, H. 1987, *Inside the Firm: The Inefficiencies of Hierarchy*, Harvard University Press.

Lele, U. 1988, 'Comparative advantage and structural

transformation: a review of Africa's economic development experience', in Ranis and Schultz (eds).

Leontief, W.W. 1953, 'Domestic production and foreign trade: the American capital position re-examined', *Proceedings of the American Philosophical Society*, 97; September. Reproduced in H.G. Johnson and R.E. Caves (eds), *Readings in International Trade*, Homewood, Ill, Irwins, 1968.

Lipsey, R.G. 1960, 'The relation between unemployment and the rate of change of money wage rates: a further analysis', *Economica*, 27; February.

Lipsey, R.G. and Lancaster, K. 1956, 'The general theory of second best', *Review of Economic Studies*, 24(1); October.

Lucas, R.E. 1976, 'Econometric policy evaluation: a critique', in K. Brunner and A. Meltzer (eds), Vol.I of Carnegie-Rochester Conference on Public Policy, a supplement to *Journal of Monetary Economics*. Amsterdam: North-Holland.

Lucas, R.E. 1977, 'Understanding business cycles', in K. Brunner and A H. Meltzer (eds), *Stabilisation of the Domestic and International Economy*. Amsterdam: North-Holland.

Lucas, R.E. and Prescott, E.C. 1971, 'Investment under uncertainty', *Econometrica*, 39(5).

Lucas, R.E. and Sargent, T.J. 1979, 'After Keynesian macroeconomics', *Federal Reserve Bank of Minneapolis Quarterly Review*, 3(2); Spring.

Lucas, R.E. and Sargent, T.J. 1981, *Rational Expectations and Econometric Practice*, University of Minneapolis Press.

McCallum, B.T. 1980, 'The significance of rational expectations theory', *Challenge*, January-February.

McKee, M. and West, E.G. 1981, 'The theory of second best: a solution in search of a problem', *Economic Inquiry*, 19(3); July.

McKinnon, R.I. 1973, *Money and Capital in Economic Development*. Washington: Brookings.

McKinnon, R.I. 1988, 'Financial liberalisation in retrospect: interest rate policies in ldcs', in Ranis and Schultz (eds).

Maddison, A. 1987, 'Growth and slowdown in advanced capitalist economies', *Journal of Economic Literature*, XXV(2); June.

Maddock, R. and Carter, M. 1982, 'A child's guide to rational expectations', *Journal of Economic Literature*, XX(1); March.

Meade, J.E. 1955, *Theory of International Economic Policy* Vol.II: *Trade and Welfare*. London: Oxford University Press.

Meade, J.E. 1982, *Stagflation*, Vol.I: *Wage Fixing*. London: Allen and Unwin.

Millward, R. 1988, 'Measured sources of inefficiency in the performance of public and private enterprises in ldcs', in Cook and Kilpatrick (eds).

Millward, R. and Parker, D. 1983, 'Public and private enterprise: comparative behaviour and relative efficiency', in R. Millward (ed), *Public Sector Economics*. London: Longman.

Moore, M. 1987, 'Interpreting Africa's crisis: political science versus political economy', *IDS Bulletin*, 18(4); October.

Myint, H. 1985, 'Organisational dualism and economic development', *Asian Development Review*, 3(1).

Nelson, R.R. and Winter, S.G. 1982, *An Evolutionary Theory of Economic Change*, Harvard University Press.

Niskanen, W.A. 1971, *Bureaucracy and Representative Government*. Chicago: Aldine-Atherton.

Perry, G.L. 1984, 'Reflections on macroeconomics', *American Economic Review*, 74(2); May.

Phelps, E. 1967, 'Phillips curves, expectations of inflation and optimal unemployment over time', *Economica*, 34; August.

Phelps, E. 1970, *Microeconomic Foundations of Employment and Inflation Theory*. New York: Norton.

Phillips, A.W. 1958, 'The relation between unemployment and the rate of change in money wage rates in the United Kingdom, 1861-1957', *Economica*, 25; November.

Rapoport, A. 1987, 'Prisoner's dilemma', in Eatwell et al (eds); Vol.3, pp.973-76.

Ranis, G. and Fei, J.C.H. 1988, 'Development economics: what next?', in Ranis and Schultz, chapter 5.

Ranis, G. and Schultz, T.P. (eds) 1988, *The State of Development Economics: Progress and Perspectives*. Oxford: Basil Blackwell.

Rashid, S. 1988, 'Economics and the study of its past', *World Development*, 16(2); February.

Reynolds, L.G. 1983, 'The spread of economic growth to the Third World, 1850-1980', *Journal of Economic Literature*, XXI(3); September.

Riddell, R.C. 1987, *Foreign Aid Reconsidered*. London: James Currey and ODI.

Rodrik, D. 1988, 'Closing the technology gap: does trade liberalization really help?' Cambridge, Massachusetts: Kennedy School, Harvard University (mimeo); May.

Roemer, M. 1985, 'Dutch disease in developing countries:

swallowing bitter medicine', in Matts Lundahl (ed), *The Primary Sector in Economic Development*. London: Croom Helm.

Ros, J. 1987, 'Growth and international trade', in Eatwell *et al,* Vol.2, pp.576-79.

Sachs, J.D. 1987, 'Trade and exchange rate policies in growth-oriented adjustment programs', in Corbo et al (eds), pp.291-352.

Sandbrook, R. 1986, 'The state and economic stagnation in tropical Africa', *World Development*, 14(3); March.

Sargent, T.J. 1982, 'Beyond demand and supply curves in macroeconomics', *American Economic Review, Papers and Proceedings*, 72(2); May.

Sargent, T.J. 1984, 'Autoregressions, expectations and advice', *American Economic Review*, 74(2); May.

Sargent, T.J. 1987, 'Rational expectations', in Eatwell et al, Vol.4, pp.76-79.

Scarf, H. 1960, 'Some examples of global instability of the competitive equilibrium', *International Economic Review*, 1; September.

Schiller, R.J. 1978, 'Rational expectations and the dynamic structure of rational expectations models: a critical review', *Journal of Monetary Economics*, 4.

Schumpeter, J.A. 1961, *Theory of Economic Development*. London and New York: Oxford University Press.

Scitovsky, T. 1954, 'Two concepts of external economies', *Journal of Political Economy*; April.

Seers, D. 1963, 'The limitations of the special case', *Bulletin of the Oxford University Institute of Economics and Statistics*, 25(2); May. Reproduced in G. M. Meier (ed), *Leading Issues in Economic Development*. New York: Oxford University Press, 1976 (3rd edition).

Sen, A.K. 1985a, 'Rationality and uncertainty', *Theory and Decision*, 18.

Sen, A.K. 1985b, 'Goals, commitment and identity', *Journal of Law, Economics and Organisation*, No.1.

Shaw, G.K. 1984, *Rational Expectations: An Elementary Exposition*. Brighton: Wheatsheaf Books.

Simon, H.A. 1982, *Models of Bounded Rationality* (2 vols). Cambridge, Massachusetts: MIT Press.

Solow, R. 1987, in 'Roundtable discussion on the Conservative Revolution', *Economic Policy*; October.

Solow, R.M. 1988, 'Growth theory and after', *American Economic Review*, 78(3); June.

Srinivasan, T.N. 1988, 'International trade and factor movements in development theory, policy and experience', in Ranis and Schultz (eds), chapter 17.

Stewart, F. 1984, 'Recent theories of international trade: some implications for the South', in Kierskowski (ed).

Stewart, F. 1985, 'The fragile foundations of the neoclassical approach to development', *Journal of Development Studies*, 21(2); January.

Stiglitz, J.E. 1986, *Economics of the Public Sector*. New York: Norton & Co.

Tinbergen, J. 1955, *On the Theory of Economic Policy*. Amsterdam: North-Holland.

Tinbergen, J. 1964, *Central Planning*. New Haven: Yale University Press.

Tinbergen, J. 1967, *Development Planning*. London: Weidenfeld and Nicolson.

Toulmin, S.E. 1950, *The Place of Reason in Ethics*, Cambridge University Press.

Toye, J. 1987, *Dilemmas of Development*. Oxford: Blackwell.

Tullock, G. 1980, 'Efficient rent seeking', in J. Buchanan, R. Tollison and G. Tullock (eds), *Towards a Theory of the Rent Seeking Society*. Texas: A. and M. University Press.

Tullock, G. 1987, 'Rent seeking', in Eatwell et al (eds); Vol.4, pp.147-49.

Van Wijnbergen, S. 1987, 'The "Dutch Disease": A disease after all?', *Economic Journal*, 94(373); March.

Venables, A.J. and Smith, A. 1986, 'Trade and industrial policy under imperfect competition', *Economic Policy*, No.3; October.

Vines, D. 1986, 'Macroeconomic policy after monetarism', *Royal Bank of Scotland Review*, 152; December.

Vines, D. 1987, 'Stabilisation policy', in Eatwell et al (eds), Vol.4, pp.464-66.

Von Weizsacker, C. 1987, in 'Roundtable discussion on the Conservative Revolution', *Economic Policy*; October.

Walsh, V. 1987, 'Philosophy and economics', in Eatwell et al, Vol.3, pp.861-69.

Wellisz, S. and Findlay, R. 1988, 'The State and the Invisible Hand', *World Bank Research Observer*, 3(1); January.

Whynes, D.K. and Bowles, R.A. 1981, *The Economic Theory of the State*. Oxford: Martin Robertson.

Williamson, J. 1985, 'Macroeconomic strategies in South America', in E. Duran (ed), *Latin America and the World Recession*, Cambridge University Press.

Williamson, O.E. 1985, *The Economic Institutions of Capitalism*. New York: Free Press.

Willig, R.D. 1987, 'Contestable markets', in Eatwell et al (eds); Vol.1, pp.618-22.

Yarrow, G. 1986, 'Privatisation in theory and practice', *Economic Policy*, No.2.

Yellen, J.L. 1984, 'Efficiency wage models of unemployment', *American Economic Review, Papers and Proceedings*, 74(2); May.